MW00582828

Time Management for College Students

How to Create Systems for Success, Exceed Your Goals, and Balance College Life

By: Discover Press

ALL RIGHTS RESERVED

No part of this book may be reproduced, stored in a retrieval system, or transmitted in any form or by any means, electronic, mechanical, photocopying, recording, scanning, or otherwise, without the prior written permission of the publisher.

Limit of Liability/Disclaimer of Warranty: the publisher and the author make no representations or warranties with respect to the accuracy or completeness of the contents of this work and specifically disclaim all warranties, including without limitation warranties of fitness for a particular purpose. No warranty may be created or extended by sales or promotional materials. The advice and strategies contained herein may not be suitable for every situation. This work is sold with the understanding that the publisher is not engaged in rendering medical, legal or other professional advice or services. If professional assistance is required, the services of a competent professional person should be sought. Neither the publisher nor the author shall be liable for damages arising herefrom. The fact that an individual, organization or website is referred to in this work as a citation and/or potential source of further information does not mean that the author or the publisher endorses the information the individuals, organization or website may provide or recommendations they/it may make. Further, readers should be aware that websites listed on this work may have changed or disappeared between when this work was written and when it is read.

Table of Contents

Introduction

What have been the biggest milestones of your life thus far? Your eighteenth birthday? A baptism? A quinceañera? A bar or bat mitzvah? No matter your culture or heritage, the transition from adolescence to adulthood is valued and celebrated.

If your eyes are glancing over the pages of this book, chances are you have reached, or are about to reach, the great milestone of having graduated high school. While this is no doubt an exciting and monumental time in your life, it is completely natural, and more than understandable, to have some doubts and concerns about what the future holds.

Maybe you are reading this book as required reading, maybe your parents want to help you get a little further ahead, or maybe you're just looking for a little guidance to ease your anxiety. Although it is my hope that you don't struggle with anxiety, I would challenge you to actually use your anxiety and doubt to your advantage.

Believe it or not, the fear that you may be experiencing is not toward the intimidation of college. You have already gotten this far; you'll be fine. As a matter of fact, it is toward the unknown. This book is not a self-help book to give you all of the answers. Rather, think of it as a trailer or a movie preview. In reading this, you'll get an idea of what you need to do in order to properly use the skills that you have already used to get this far. My hope is that this book empowers you to be able to identify just what these tools are and to hone in on them. Your tools are your own, and no two people work the exact same way. Anyone that tells you they have a "fool-proof method that anyone can use" is probably trying to sell you something.

Let's look at the fact that you are going to college. That demonstrates one of two things: you are motivated to be successful in life, or you are being supported by people that want you to succeed. With that in mind, what are you going to do with your new collegiate life? What are your goals? I hope it is not simply to get a degree and move on with your life. Barely scraping by with straight-C's sounds like a pretty miserable way to experience college, doesn't it? That is a waste of time and money for everyone involved.

Instead, you should be starting to consider more than simply what your major will be. These questions can all be categorized under one bigger question: "What do I want my life to look like?" While no one has total control over their life, considering what you would like to do with your social life is important, as well as whether or not you want to pursue romance.

I'm sure there were times in high school where you felt that you were transitioning into being an adult, and you absolutely were. As stated, the tools you either did or did not develop will carry over. However, high school was a heavily regulated and supervised environment. If you struggled in a certain area, you may have had a concerned loved one or teacher step in and try to help you after observing that struggle.

While there are plenty of supports for you in college, you have to take the initiative to seek out the help in order to receive it. If you do not advocate for yourself, you will be held accountable when things are either not completed or done incorrectly.

This is not meant to scare or intimidate you. The entire purpose of college, beyond the more apparent objective of academic success, is to help you transition to the tough realities of the world. However, despite the world being tough, there is a fairness to a system of consequences because there are also rewards. My hope, again, is that you mature into someone who can see what tools you have used to get this far and what tools you still need to develop.

As stated, your tools are your own. You should be personalizing everything to make yourself the most successful and efficient in all that you do. With that said, it is important to keep in mind that the skills and methods you utilize to complete a task may be completely foreign and confusing to some others, regardless of how obvious and simple your way may seem to you.

Additionally, no two colleges are exactly the same. One reader may be attending a grand state university on an enormous campus while the next may be going to a small local community college, and still the next may be enrolled in an online college. All three are excellent pursuits, and no one should feel inferior or superior based on their soon-to-be alma mater. It is, however, important to consider that these three common settings will offer a different set of resources for students. Additionally, surrounding towns are going to differ vastly, especially for the online students who could be attending from literally anywhere with Internet access. For these reasons, this book will be universally valuable and applicable, regardless of the format and setting of your learning.

Up to this point, this entire introduction has made the assumption that you are already either attending or enrolled in a college. Some of you reading this may be working on applications to a number of schools. Perhaps you are considering which of the college settings listed above would work best for both you and your finances. After all, trillions of dollars are owed nationally in student loan debt, and I'm sure you do not want to fall any deeper into debt than you have to.

If you find yourself in this searching stage, look into some components of the college that you may not have considered before, such as the community surrounding the campus (if attending in-person), the demographics of the student body culture, any interesting clubs or extracurricular opportunities for attendees, and maybe even the quality of food that is served at the campus cafeteria and/or restaurants on-site. Some schools may have an excellent program in the field of your interest but lack in these other areas. Wondering whether or not your future school's gymnasium has a racquetball court, or to see if there is a major city within an hour drive of the campus are perfectly legitimate checklist items that may very well cross off some seemingly perfect schools or programs.

In starting this book off, a good way to start your collegiate career may be to arrive at the school early. Some schools even offer a free class for incoming freshman during the summer. Arriving early is not only a good opportunity to start getting to know people, but it would help you get settled in with some of the technicalities such as your devices getting onto Wi-Fi, obtaining all of your textbooks ahead of the rush, having a relaxed opportunity to explore the surrounding area, learning about the student resources offered to you, finding good study spots, and figuring out any other things you are interested in. Making the objective to settle in comfortably before classes begin will help give some peace of mind and a major advantage while starting in a new place.

Finally, keep in mind that despite the title of this book having the phrase "Time Management" in it, there is so much more that it has to offer than just a few tips on how to get stuff done. Professional success may be a desire for students, which is likely if collegiate-level education is being pursued. Unfortunately, success and happiness are not positively correlated. In fact, many of the most successful people are unhappy. Professional and financial fortune do not guarantee satisfaction with life, as many people have to neglect their personal lives and family time in order to achieve the former. The main purpose of this book is to help establish healthy standards and discipline for yourself, and being able to manage time is merely one of these components.

This book is divided into three main parts. Part I will deal with "Creating Systems for Success." Essentially, this portion will focus on easy and accessible ways in which you can make the most out of your collegiate environment. This is not only in reference to campus life since, as stated, many people attend college online. Nevertheless, whether you reside at your school or your school resides with you, every student has some sort of a collegiate environment, so making the most out of it will be the primary objective of the first portion.

Next, the second portion is entitled "Exceed Your Goals." Everybody talks about the value of "accomplishing goals," but what does that look like? How do you accomplish goals if you don't know how to set them? This section will provide a little insight on a common way to set easy and achievable goals, and then what to do once they've been set.

Finally, the third section is focused on the seemingly impossible task to "Balance College Life." This portion will discuss the importance of determining your priorities and values, and how to balance all of them through the ability to dedicate time to all of them.

College may be different for everyone, but the objective of multifaceted growth and development remains universal. My hope is that reading this will help you develop the tools you already have and make them work to their fullest potential. Now that we have established the objectives for this book, let's get started.

Part I: Creating Systems for Success

Chapter 1: Who You Know

Many people have used the phrase, "It's not what you know. It's who you know." What does this even mean?
The basic idea of the phrase is that one's success is not actually based on ability, talent, intelligence, or even merit. Rather, the alleged more important attribute for a person to get ahead in the world is being "well connected," and having a strong network of people to help. More so, the people in this theoretical network are powerful enough to get you a good job. This phrase is actually often used in contexts where it seems as if someone got a good position NOT based on their abilities, only because they know someone high enough up the ladder. Sometimes it just pokes fun at people who are blatantly bad at their job.

Is there any truth to this saying? Well, yes, to some extent.

When searching for work, especially in the professional realm, references are such a pivotal part of the hiring process. Being able to list people who are able to provide positive feedback on your past work is often the determination of whether or not you will be hired, and rightfully so! A potential employer should not assume that a prospect hire is being completely transparent and honest on their resume. Additionally, a job listing on one's work history does not guarantee that the job was completed honestly, thoroughly, or even necessarily well at all. For these reasons, it is important to start working on developing a strong network as soon as possible.

Another reason that references are so important in finding work is that it demonstrates an ability to communicate. One's ability to network and engage in a professional relationship with multiple people is an important trait in so many work environments. While there is nothing wrong with having more of a shy personality, a proper communicator has a significant advantage over someone that is less inclined to meet new people. Proving that one has the ability to reach out and engage with others may determine or defer one's success, depending on the particular professional environment.

Some college or high school students may hear this advice and shrug it off, thinking that it is not relevant to them since they do not work. Maybe some are working small jobs and do not feel like a reference from their current work would be helpful in the future. On the contrary, it is extremely invaluable for a young person to be able to establish themselves with the reputation of being a hard worker early on. Do not look down on any strong reference!

How does this apply to your education? Believe it or not, your professors can serve as legitimate professional references. Many jobs even appreciate receiving a reference from an instructor, especially if they instructed a class within your chosen field of study. Although the thought may seem intimidating, you have nothing to fear in approaching a professor. In fact, you may be surprised at how pleasant it can be to find common ground with a professor and strike up a conversation before or after class. If you encounter a professor who is less friendly or engaging, maybe even showing little interest in chatting, don't let it get you down. There are plenty of great professors at your school. It is almost inevitable that you will have notably good, notably bad, and notably forgettable professors during your college career, just as you have throughout your entire education.

What makes a good or bad professor? This is a difficult question as different people will likely have their own answers to share based on past experiences. Nevertheless, there are a few common traits that most people would probably find relatable and agreeable.

First, a good professor has your academic success in mind. No matter how tough things get, you cannot blame a professor for teaching difficult subject matter. However, you can blame them if you express a need for help, and they are not willing to provide you with some clarification or even refer you to resources that can better assist you. Having an instructor take time out of their personal lives to personally tutor you cannot be expected, and is quite rare, so one's inability to do so should not be held against them either. It is not uncommon for a professor to begin a semester by reviewing the syllabus and posting their open-door office hours in order to schedule time, sometimes even just to walk straight in. For a bad professor, this would involve a lack of responsiveness or interest in your expressed needs. Maybe they choose not to have office hours or refuse to respond to any inquiries outside of the classroom. This can be fine, as long as some level of communication or assistance is offered.

Along with this point, it is worth calling back to this book's introduction, which explains how college students need to advocate for themselves and not rely on people to come help them. In judging a professor's quality, make sure that you are reaching out if you are struggling.

Additionally, a good professor engages with the class instead of reciting what is practically a script. While teachers are required to have a curriculum for their classes, and are expected to stick with it, a great teacher is one who is able to do so while simultaneously opening up the opportunity for the class to be engaged and expressive. Along with this, what seems to be a common trait amongst well-liked professors is their ability to utilize or tolerate humor during the lecture. Doing so does not mean that they do not take the subject matter seriously. Rather, it may actually be a sign they are so competent and confident in what they are teaching that they are willing to keep things light-hearted.

Author's Experience

Whether or not you have studied psychology as your major, you probably wouldn't be surprised to hear that some teachers love to get into the heads of their students! One of the most respected and intimidating professors on my college's campus worked in the psychology department and, as a psych major myself, I was naturally terrified of taking her courses. She was so distinguished that everyone thought that she was

13

the head of the department. She was not, which only goes to show how important and respected she was.

When the dreaded time came to take the first course with her, everyone was practically wetting their pants as she regally and quietly walked into the room. Her first words only came after putting her books down on the desk and, as she fixed her posture and confidently raised her stoic face, she projected, "GOOD MORNING, CLASS!" Everyone uniformly responded, "Good morning!" Despite this dramatic introduction, she proceeded to interject humor into her lectures, though the respect and intimidation were present up until graduation day, all throughout the three courses that she taught.

Even as my fellow psychology majors and I were sitting in the department's pre-graduation ceremony, we were still whispering to one another, "Do you think we passed?! Did we graduate?! I don't know! I'm so nervous!" Almost telepathically knowing this, the good doctor proceeded to the podium for her commencement speech, looked each of us square in the eye (somehow simultaneously), and simply said, "Students, you made it. It's over," with such a beautiful smile on her face. All of us sighed and slouched in our benches.

I have a plethora of stories about this professor, about the times where I was so stressed that I didn't think I'd make it, about helping some of my classmates through their anxiety attacks while working on group projects, about how it was so difficult to schedule office hours because of everyone clawing for one-on-one time with her. At the end of the day, I don't quickly recall the blood, sweat, and tears. Rather, I look back on how much she taught all of us, and about how she didn't waste any of her words during lectures. In fact, I used to liken her to Mr. Miyagi from *The Karate Kid* to one of my classmates. Said friend agreed so much that she purchased me a figure of Daniel from the film as a symbol of having made it to graduation. Despite being so respected and feared, I think back on her as an amazing, brilliant, kind-hearted, and wonderfully humorous woman who cared so much about both her students and the subject matter that she taught.

Along with connecting to your professors, it can be just as important, even more so in some cases, to find a quality academic advisor. The general role of an advisor is to help direct you toward taking the courses that help you complete your requirements for your desired degree. However, if the task of being an advisor were this simple, then you could simply look at your degree audit and see what classes you have to take. Rather, a good advisor will help you take generals and major-focused courses that will help you gain experience in your desired career path. For instance, if you are a journalism major but have an interest in writing, your advisor might suggest that you take on English as your minor area of study. Maybe you are planning on heading toward a career in the field of mathematics, but you have always wanted to open your own small business. A proper advisor should suggest that you take a few specific business classes in order to help you achieve that goal someday. This idea just goes back to college being so much more than just getting a degree, and an advisor that really cares can help you accomplish some of the dreams that may have seemed silly at one point or another.

Just as was stated about professors being able to serve as legitimate references, it is even better if you are able to have an advisor serve as one. Doing so has the potential of communicating to a potential employer that you are heading in the direction that your advisor assisted you with. Additionally, listing an advisor shows that some level of reliable, consistent communication with a resource took place, as one does not often have multiple academic advisors once they have chosen a major area of study.

One other characteristic that a good advisor would demonstrate in the right circumstance is to make the tough and uncomfortable move toward redirecting a student that may have an unreasonable or unrealistic career path. How difficult would it be to tell someone excited about something that their joy and motivation is not reasonable? Unfortunately, there are plenty of starry-eyed students who have unrealistic ideas and visions of how their life ought to be. An advisor is an advocate, and being an advocate often means getting your hands dirty and trying to redirect someone into a more reasonable direction. Just as people say of friendship, a true friend is willing to be honest, even when it's not easy to do so.

Along with connecting to professors and advisors, one of your greatest assets as a student is connecting with reliable and honest classmates, preferably in the same major as yourself. You would be surprised at how close you and your cohort of classmates can become as you all traverse through the required courses together. The last "Author's Experience" blurb mentions a close working relationship with a classmate. That classmate and I used to work on pretty much every paper we had together during our last year in the psychology

16

program. The tougher things got, the more frequently we would be on a web call, go out to a local diner, or just meet up on campus and work on our own projects. This is not to say that we would work together on one paper and submit the same body of work. Rather, it became more about having a second set of eyes and/or ears to bounce ideas off of for our own respective projects, and make sure that neither one of us was losing our own minds along the way. If not for her and our ability to put our minds together, I am honestly not too sure if I would have successfully made it through.

Finding someone like-minded in your field should not be too difficult. After all, the other people in your department were led in the same academic direction, and it would be surprising if you shared absolutely no personality traits with any of them! Additionally, one of the amazing components of being a college student at this time in history is that races, ethnicities, nationalities, sexual orientations, and other paths of life are not excluded from enrollment. Although this may be something that anyone growing up in the current society might take for granted, segregation and exclusion was not long ago, so today's college students have an amazing opportunity to intertwine with people not only from all over the country, but from all over the world as well. Taking full advantage of this and learning about different cultures and approaches is absolutely invaluable to growing an open mind. Furthermore, within all of this diversity, it is far from impossible to find people with similar personalities to your own that you can pair up with.

If none of these ideas of teaming up work for you, and you would prefer to just work on your projects alone, there is absolutely nothing wrong with that. In fact, showing some independence with your assignments is very important. The only thing that you should keep in mind is if this is more applicable to you, there are times where you may feel alone, as if there are not many people, if anyone, who can relate to whatever academic struggles you are going through. If you insist on not collaborating with any of your collegiate colleagues, consider just having a friend to talk to if and when things become difficult. In Alcoholics Anonymous, there is a buddy system in place that has participants find a sponsor. This is another attendee who, ideally, has a similar mindset and/or personality to yourself. The system does not demand or even recommend that everything be done together. Rather, it provides individuals a contact to reach out to when things become difficult, especially when sobriety starts to feel like a daunting and impossible climb. The role of the sponsor is to provide advice and encouragement when their partner is fighting the temptation to run to the liquor store and surrender their battle. Likewise, having a sponsor-type figure in your academic life can provide some much-needed support, and should ideally be someone within your chosen field of study. Although it does not have to be, having someone who is either going through the same courses as you or has already passed the courses provides a sense of relatability and better allows your "sponsor" to relate to the struggles that you are going through.

There are plenty of other groups of people to connect with outside of the ones mentioned in this portion. Students, teachers, and advisors certainly are not the only demographics of people that you will encounter when attending in-person or online college. Some professors have teaching assistants, on-site colleges have employees in their restaurants or cafeterias, administrative staff who handle finances and enrollment traditionally work on the school's grounds, dormitories usually have multiple deans employed, and other people on campus you can talk to. Being able to meet a new person and create a personal, professional, or romantic relationship is a fundamental part of the human experience and, thankfully, college is an incredibly helpful and diverse environment to further develop this skill. Take full advantage of the different personalities, professions, and demographics that are on your campus or attending your online classes.

Chapter 2: Get a Job!

The last chapter discussed the importance of finding strong connections while attending college. One of the major points brought up was the ability to meet people and develop a network of reliable references in order to pursue a good job after graduation.

What now? Many college students work throughout their collegiate careers. After all, college tuition isn't cheap, and getting ahead on a mountain of student loans is imperative to avoid being in debt for the rest of your life. It does not matter that you cannot afford to pay the whole tuition each month or each year in total. Any bit of it being paid is helpful and is less money that will need to be paid back later. Additionally, it is less money that will build interest as a loan, so getting started early is essential.

Okay, so building references and knocking out some debt are two significant reasons why one should work in college, but what about those whose parents or scholarships are taking care of tuition? What about the people that have so much studying to do that there seems to be little to no time to work and earn some money? Fair enough. Everyone has different circumstances that may prevent them from part-time work during their collegiate careers. Nevertheless, there is still an interjection for such individuals, and it can be summarized in one word: experience.

There are two major criteria when hiring an individual: their education and their past experience. Yes, your education is obviously very important. After all, it is the very reason why you are in school! You would like to live a happy and comfortable life, and the current job market is very competitive. Having a degree from a strong and legitimate school is an important factor in securing a solid and stable career. However, your candidacy as a potential new hire will drop substantially if you have no experience in your chosen field outside of reading textbooks and writing papers.

Many, if not most, collegiate programs require at least one internship or field placement within their curriculum. For obvious reasons, it is an easy way for students to gain experience within their chosen field of study. Going beyond just the experience and firsthand exposure, participating in an internship is actually a legitimate addition to your resume. Unfortunately, not every program requires an extensive internship, and some only require a small number of hours to graduate. This is a perfect opportunity for you to look for work, regardless of whether or not it is within your chosen area of study. Should you find a job in your chosen field, then that is excellent. You may even be able to assign it as your internship when the time comes, usually further into your college experience. Either way, even if it is in a different area or on your college campus, just having any work experience is an excellent way to spend your time in college.

As stated before, some students find themselves with absolutely no time to work or even to relax, as there are so many studies that consume all of their time. Some people make claims that "there is always time," but for some, having no time is unfortunately a legitimate reality. Medical students, such as pre-nursing or pre-med studies, have so much on their plates that there is little to no room to even breathe. Such students must actually complete rounds later within their programs, so this section is less applicable to such individuals. However, there are still plenty of students who are completely consumed by their respective programs. Maybe they have even chosen to take on a double major and are handling double the workload of a normal student.

The blessing of being a college student in this day and age is the increased opportunities that come with the Internet. Students who need a job should look to see what remote options are available based on factors such as past experience, past education, current education, future plans, and personal talents and interests. Believe it or not, many employers (particularly in more professional environments) are actually interested to find out what kinds of things you enjoy doing in your spare time. They may ask what you read, watch, or even what you feel you are most talented at doing. All of these factors could play a role in helping you gain experience.

In addition to seeing what is available online, look to see what jobs are available at your school if you attend in-person and/or live on campus. Not having a long commute is a major influencer in being able to find the time to work while being a full-time student in college. Many positions are needed on the weekends when students are less motivated to work, and there may not even be extensive time slots that would consume too much of your social life.

Author's Experience

During my first year in college, I was anxious to get a job, though my parents were adamant about me taking the time to get adjusted to the new environment before I did so. Once my second year came around, I was hired to work at the small grocery store on my college campus. It was convenient geographically, as it was just across the street from the dormitory I resided in, so getting to and from work was very handy.

While I was grateful for the opportunity to start getting work experience to add to my lack of resume, even making just a little bit of money as well, it was a nightmare of a job. The work itself was not too bad, but my boss was insufferable to be around. He was rude, lazy, and overly critical when I would complete the very tasks that he did not train me to do. I did everything that I could to keep positive and work hard. However, after a year of silent frustration, I caved in and snapped back at my boss one day. One should never do this, no matter how rough the job gets, and I was admittedly afraid of the repercussions, even though it was just a quick "OKAY, I GET IT!" Thankfully, instead of terminating my position, he apologized, and I did as well. I got out of this situation by good fortune, as another boss would have fired me on the spot.

Although my boss and I seemed to get past this incident, my dad was coincidentally visiting that day, and I spoke with him about the incident. Very simply, I told him that I did not have a choice but to find another job. Fortunately, he was surprisingly understanding of my frustration, and allowed me to give my two weeks' notice, even though I did not have another job lined up. The next day, I put in my two weeks' notice for the first time in my life. Funnily enough, my boss was the nicest he had ever been over those weeks and kept expressing how much he had appreciated my working there.

Once my time had finished at the grocery store, I made it my mission to find a better, more professional job. This proved to be difficult, as my only experience had been a small job or two I had done in high school, along with the job I had just left, so there was not much work history to boast. Finally, a few weeks later, I found a job in the enrollment department of my school and could not have been happier. It even proved to be a job that I continued until graduation, having been asked to serve another role in the department after my position was eliminated. Going back to the value of a strong reference, I even asked one of my bosses in the enrollment department to serve as a job reference four and a half years after I graduated college.

I realize that there have been repetitive examples of jobs and getting references, but keep in mind that the subject of this section revolves around "Creating Systems for Success." By talking back to my boss, regardless of how rude and disrespectful he was being to me, having gotten fired from my first collegiate job would not have looked good on my record; and I would have had to explain what had happened to each potential employer in the future, as many interviewers and applications ask, "Have you ever been terminated from a position?" If the subject of "Creating Systems for Success" is being discussed, it is equally as important to present the potential of sabotaging said success.

Much of this section has emphasized the importance of proper references in gaining strength in your career. However, it is worth noting that your behavior in your jobs, your classes, and on campus (if in-person) is invaluable. Demonstrating not just a sense of professionalism, but a sense of self-control and public composure is essential in letting your superiors know that you want to develop and uphold a good reputation for yourself. Just to be clear: in no way does this imply that you have to be uptight and serious all the time. No one genuinely and consistently enjoys the company of people with absolutely no sense of humor that are never able to loosen up or have fun. It's probably safe to say that we all know someone like that, and they are insufferable!

Professionalism is not as comically serious and straitlaced as it is portrayed in the media. Rather, it is more about being yourself and natural while also respecting the social environment that you are in. For example: most would agree that there is nothing wrong with sharing a dirty joke with your friends; but sharing it with your colleagues at work could potentially be interpreted as sexual harassment. Vice versa, formally scheduling a meeting with a superior is generally protocol instead of popping into someone's office, yet it would seem awkward to be so formal with your friends, and it may come across as socially uncomfortable to be so uptight.

These examples might seem painfully on-the-nose, but what it comes down to is that some people actually struggle to know their boundaries between environments. There are still countless men who see absolutely no issue in sharing a dirty joke or flirting with a female coworker in the middle of the workplace. Additionally, if you grew up with little social interaction or if you struggle with a social disorder, basic casual interactions are a daunting barrier that do not come quickly or naturally. For those with said disorder, social interactions have to be consciously learned, which is not as easy or simple as watching and observing. Even for those more severe cases where proper guidance, treatment, therapy, coaching, and even some supportive friends are all present, the interactions themselves are still somewhat awkward and uncomfortable, even if more confidence is felt by the individual. Although these points and examples are being shared to emphasize the importance of knowing your social environment, consider the side note of not jumping to oversimplified conclusions about someone being "weird." You do not know what struggles an individual has gone through, or is still going through.

Back to the point: try to gauge your audience. The environments of the workplace and interactions with friends were given, though there are plenty more examples to select from. For instance, would you act the same way around your significant other's family as you do when you two are alone or on a date? Hopefully not, as intimacy goes so far beyond physicality. Hopefully, the time you share alone is full of love and affection, expressed and shared between you both. As beautiful as young love is, not everybody wants to see it. Save your PDA for another time, not when you are with your family or that of your significant other.

In all of these same ways, save the casualness for outside of the workplace. Dress appropriately, follow the rules, and keep a happy and relaxed demeanor about you while consistently respecting those around you. As simple as those behaviors sound, it still takes practice not to slip and let a dirty joke slide, or to sidetrack a work-related conversation to talk about a movie you just saw. The truth and reality of it all is that your boss may very well engage in these behaviors, which may seem like a free pass to do it yourself. Fight that temptation! Go ahead and engage in the fun dialogue with your boss, and keep things light if the environment calls for it, but keep things professional on your end. If you play your cards right, you have the potential of being the likable and fun boss that everyone dreams of having.

Chapter 3: Find Your Zone

Despite this book being about collegiate life, so little of the actual academics have been discussed. What is college without the books, assignments, quizzes, tests, and other methods of learning?

Depending on your program, much of undergraduate college involves quizzes and testing, where graduate school is more centered around reports and papers in general. As an undergraduate college student, it is essential for you to learn your own best ways of "getting into the zone." Well, what does this mean?

Have you ever heard of this phrase? It can be used with just about any context that involves some sort of concentration and focus. Some people might call it getting hyped or amped up, though that's more related to when someone needs adrenaline. Rather, this is more about shutting off the world around you and honing in on the material before you.

This section will do its best to not lecture you on how to study. After all, you figured out how to get through high school. Even though college is more challenging than high school for the most part, at least requiring more out of students, the habits that you have established up until this point will certainly continue. Unfortunately, this also applies to people who may have slacked their way through high school, taking every shortcut to simply get by. Having said that, there is absolutely nothing wrong with making your work more efficient.

All in all, it's probably safe to say that most people reading this book know the difference between efficient working and slacking off. It is also probably safe to assume that most students reading this also know what it's like to be "in the zone," though it may be presumptuous to conclude that you all have it down to an art. Never in your lives has it been more essential to find your zone, as you will have to figure out a way to be able to do it almost every single day.

More so now, it is worth reiterating one of the main points in the introduction that nothing in this book, especially this section, is absolute. The only thing that this author can do is share what I have learned for myself. This book's purpose is to inspire students to develop their own ways of succeeding. In sharing perspectives, the intention is not to lecture or promote "sure-fire" ways toward success. Rather, the point is for you to read this and find inspiration within yourselves. After all, this is why the book's phrasing speaks directly to you, not to a figurative audience.

Okay, now that the disclaimers and sappy sentiments are out of the way, let's help you find your zone!

First, one of the most important elements of being in the zone is your environment: your literal, nonfigurative zone. Where are you choosing to go to study or complete assignments? You should have at least two or three go-to places that are very different from one another. These should be places that are either quiet or promote a sense of peace. I'm sure that a few places had to have come to your mind. A coffee shop, student lounge/s, a peaceful outdoor area, a cafeteria, a favorite restaurant or diner, and a miscellaneous public building with seating are some immediate ideas that come to mind.

How about the most obvious one: a library? Most, if not all, colleges have libraries for the campus. Even the smallest of towns have some form of a library in their downtown area. How perfect is a library when you need a quiet space? There are literally people on staff to shut people up if they talk! Unfortunately, this is only perfect in theory. Some libraries do absolutely nothing to keep the peace. While college is great for having people from all different walks of life, the downside of diversity is that it brings about various personalities, which include people with no consideration for others. These people apparently have nothing better to do than to pester people around them by talking on the phone or even talking to others who are just as inconsiderate as they are; and yet, all of these conversations tend to be about absolutely nothing whatsoever!

Joking aside, let's be real: have we not all had these frustrated thoughts and annoyances in the past? You're probably wondering why that rant was so harsh. Essentially, it was exaggerated for laughs, but it evokes the frustration of when you're trying to study, and others around you aren't being considerate; so as a side note, don't be this person. On the other hand, believe it or not, you have complete and total control over whether or not you will subject yourself to these annoyances. One of the first things you ought to do when starting at a school is explore what areas work best for you.

Most environments are fairly consistent with their noise levels, so get a feel for what you like.

Weirdly enough, an environment's study appeal goes beyond just its sonic qualities. Small factors are just as important: the comfort of seating, desk space, even the wall colors and furnishings. Is the lighting fluorescent and cold or incandescent and warm? Does this selected environment allow room and space for others to join you if studying in a group? Does the space offer free Wi-Fi or Ethernet spots? Does it require a reservation or cost money to be there, such as a rented room in a library or a local eatery? There is nothing wrong with hitting up a diner and getting refillable coffee for $2.00, but that money eventually adds up. If you went every day for a year, it would cost you $730.00, and that's more than any college student should be spending on much of anything!

This may seem like an obvious point, but make sure that this space is easily accessible on a whim. If you don't have a car to drive somewhere, your spot needs to be in walking distance. Furthermore, make it close so that you do not have far to walk if the weather becomes inclement or if you have a personal emergency. If you live on a campus, you should explore every single department's building, not just your own. In the same way that general classes give you a sample of what each area of study has to offer, take the time to see how each department arranges their respective areas of space.

Author's Experience

During my first year, and for a few scattered semesters throughout my whole time in college, I did not have a car at my disposal. On top of that, when I did, it was always parked at my sister's dormitory and, later on, her on-campus apartment. This meant that I had to coordinate using it with her. Although she was never remotely greedy with it and always encouraged me to use it, I would have to walk across campus to retrieve it. On top of that, our campus was built on the side of a large hill, so on my laziest days or on rainy days, it never seemed worth it.

All of this meant that I had to find spaces on-campus that I could focus in, and this proved to be a daunting task. My dormitory had tables and chairs scattered throughout the building, though the noise levels and ungodly stenches from nearby rooms made these options unfeasible. My own room was impossible to study in since my stranger roommate was a weirdly ripped hillbilly that would go to bed at around 5:30 or 6:00 every evening. The one night I tried studying in there with a small desk lamp on, he nagged me until I had to leave.

The library was a joke of a study space. My self-aware rant about people in the library talking, although written to be humorous, was one that I could relate to. I'd even respectfully ask people to be quiet, and I'd get chewed out. At that point, I did not have a major, and found myself exploring each building to find the best study space. Eventually, I found myself most content with the cafeteria in between meals when it was empty. There were a few small tables by the large windows, which allowed for natural light and, even despite the dated décor of the large room, having a nice view overlooking the campus consumed most of my view. Having a table to myself allowed me to spread my books and papers out, and the

32

lack of anyone except the cafeteria staff made it more than quiet.

Once my sister graduated and I had the car to myself, I also embraced a psychology major and began to collaborate with friends, so we would meet and work together on almost every paper. This became a great experience, as they would recommend their favorite study spots, most of which I had not come across in my searching. Additionally, when we would decide to go into the community, we would all take turns driving so that we would save on gas expenses. It just goes to show that the signs of a good study team go so far beyond the academic components.

During the entirety of my time in college, my friends and I used to frequent a diner that was about fifteen minutes from the school's campus. A close friend and I went there several times a week during the semester that he and I were roommates, especially on evenings where one of us was particularly frustrated about something and we needed a chance to vent to one another. This quickly became one of my favorite, if not my favorite, restaurants in the area. Once I reached my last year in the psychology program and my senior thesis approached, I found myself going to this diner almost every night. The waitstaff came to know me, and there were nights where I wouldn't even have to get anything there beyond free glasses of water. I chose for my senior thesis to partially focus on the life and philosophies of Fred "Mister" Rogers, and his impact on the field of psychology overall. One of the best parts of getting to write this paper was having to watch clips and episodes of *Mister Rogers' Neighborhood* in order to find the answers to some of the preplanned questions. As I researched and wrote, the servers at the diner would get so excited to see Mister Rogers on my computer screen while they walked by and would ask how my paper had been going every time I would come in.

This diner proved to be the ultimate study space for me. I would study there alone or with my classmate as we worked on our respective projects together. Even though it took me years to find how well it worked for me, it came through for me at the most important time of my collegiate career. It was a consistently reliable place that had quiet music, considerate customers, pleasing aesthetic furnishings, perfect lighting, and the tables had great space for spreading out. If I became hungry, the food was excellent and cheap, and I could get as much coffee as I wanted for about a dollar. Find your space and make it your zone.

Okay, great: you've finally found your favorite spots to study and write in. What now? This conversation starts to shift toward calling back to the conveniences of modern technology. You have so many options on your phone, tablet, and computer, and access to the Internet opens up even more possibilities and services. If you enjoy listening to music to help you focus, Spotify, iTunes/Apple Music, YouTube Music, Pandora, and so many other services offer you the ability to curate your own playlists and radio stations to meet your stylistic needs. If you don't find a free service that you prefer using, it is not uncommon to find a service that also offers a student discount, and paying a few dollars a month is substantially cheaper than buying albums or individual songs. A lot of great styles of music to consider include more traditional styles of classical and jazz, or more modern types such as lo-fi. It is generally best to listen to something that you are not completely familiar with, rather something that simply sets the mood. Your mind needs to be relaxed, not having another distraction to take you away from your studies.

Oddly enough, and this point will likely seem very obvious, but consider what you are wearing when you sit down to study. Beyond the benefits and luxuries of modern technology, the current social norms promote comfort in stylistic trends. How fortunate we are to be living in a time where sweats, gym clothes, and yoga pants are considered proper attire for going into public. Take advantage of this! Get comfortable in some (clean) sweats and find your zone in comfort.

How clean is your living space? This is not as related to having a place to study, just in general. Are there clothes, dirty or clean, piling up on every conceivable surface? Do empty food and drink containers cover what was once the floor? Is the utilization of the trash can or recycling bin more of a suggestion than a mandate? Regardless of whether you choose to study here or not, try to keep your residence clean, or at least somewhat organized. Remember: college is a time for growth, and "growth" goes so far beyond just academic success. Take advantage of having your own space and learn to manage it. If you cannot keep a small dormitory room or bedroom clean, how can you expect to keep a whole apartment or house clean in the future?

With this said, it is worth acknowledging that different people and different personalities thrive in different environments. There are certainly a large number of people that find "organized chaos" to be more productive than actual organization. Fair enough. However, ask yourself: would you want someone you respect to see your space? Would your mother, father, grandparents, or even just your friends want to spend time with you in a space where you have to crab walk to avoid stepping on anything? Should you find yourself pursuing a career within a professional environment, keep in mind that any cubicle or office space has to be kept clean and organized. Having piles of junk everywhere, even just papers, is completely unacceptable.

Why is this? Essentially, it demonstrates to other professionals that you lack basic organizational skills, regardless of whether you know where everything is or not. It reflects that you are incapable of order and discipline for yourself; and if you cannot discipline yourself, how can you expect to manage others if given more authority? This all may seem superficial, but there is some honest truth to it. How many times in your life have you gotten into someone's car and internally made assumptions and judgements over how dirty it was? Burger wrappers on the dashboards, miscellaneous trash on the floor, stale French fries under the seat, discolored crumbs in the cupholders. We've all experienced something like this, and it is not comfortable for anyone except the car's owner, who has grown familiar with this. This type of car setting certainly would not be accepted for any Uber or Lyft driver. Would you not feel more welcomed in a nice and clean car with vacuumed floors and mats? Try to utilize this time in your life to keep the little space you have clean and organized, and see if it makes a difference in how your friends and your peers respect you.

Considering how busy you are with your academic work, with your social life, and with your job if you have one, how do you manage keeping clean with the little time you have? Actually, it can be quite simple. Staying organized or messy is often contingent on one key factor: how much stuff you own. Do you have too many clothing items? Do you keep every trinket, keychain, and souvenir that people have bought for you over the years? Do you struggle to throw away papers and documents that you don't need anymore? Is there just an overall struggle to dispose of things you no longer use, whatever that may include?

Should you decide to keep a simple, clean, and organized space, the key to success is differentiating between "want" and "need." With clothes in particular, you could even change these terms to "use" and "don't use." There are so many places to donate clothes, and doing so would be a great way to give to someone who would use it instead of having it just sit in your closet and take up space. Some places, such as Plato's Closet, even purchase certain clothing items, so consider making a little money off of what you already have! Selling clothes on Facebook Marketplace is another opportunity to make some extra cash.

When it comes to miscellaneous items, think of a ratio of storage and all personal belongings. Of course, there are opportunities to reorganize and purchase more storage bins or drawers, but there comes a point in time where you eventually run out of space in your living arrangement. The easy solution for papers and documents is to scan them and store them on your electronic device. Smartphones and tablets have free applications and features where you can simply take a picture of a document and save it as a PDF file. Backing these up on a hard drive and then shredding the physical copy is a quick and reliable way to ensure that you have these documents forever. With any other items, try to put sentiment aside, or designate a small storage area for cards you appreciate or small gifts you would like to keep. Consider even asking your parents if they have storage room for such items. Otherwise, keep the storage to possessions ratio in mind as you try to maintain a clean living space. If everything that you need has a designated space, and you discipline yourself to put things back after you use them, the time it will take to clean will be a small maintenance, not a chore.

Author's Experience

As I was preparing to room with one of my close friends, I asked another close friend who had known my future roommate his whole life if this rooming situation would work. He stated that this new roommate emulates and reflects whatever cleaning behaviors the other roommate does; if I am clean, then he will be clean, and vice versa. This assessment made sense to me, so I went through with it.

My other friend's feedback could not have been more accurate. We had a great time as roommates, and almost always had a consistently clean and organized room. He and I pitched in to get a small coffee maker and kept it on our dorm room sink area. This room was so inviting that our RA (Resident Assistant) would burst into the room like Kramer on "Seinfeld" and welcome himself to a cup of coffee whenever he wanted, and we invited him to do so. This RA and I later became very good friends, and even had an apartment together the following year.

This roommate and I are close friends to this day. We all moved back to our home state and have our own respective lives. My former roommate lives with a few friends in a house and, unfortunately, my other friend's assessment remains true. The friends that my former roommate lives with are absolutely disgusting in the way that they maintain their living space, and my friend does not maintain cleanliness either, despite being the owner of the house. This has gotten out of hand to the point where it is hard for me and my significant other to go visit it in its current state. We are close enough friends to where I felt inclined to bring this matter up to him in private, complimenting his potential that I saw while living with him. He was so receptive to having heard this, and he even thanked me, saying that it was something that he needed to hear.

I saw my friend a week or so after we had engaged in this conversation. He told me with pride that he put his foot down toward one of his housemates during the past week, and had demanded that he clean up after himself in the kitchen. He went on to say that his roommate "played dumb" at first, acting as if he had simply forgotten to wash his dishes, and immediately started cleaning.

On a separate note, keep in mind as you begin college that being a good friend sometimes means having difficult conversations with people. If you truly care about someone in your life, it takes more than simply having fun with them. Being willing and able to have a difficult conversation may just prove to be something that someone needed to hear, especially if they respect and care about you as well.

Chapter 4: Life Outside the Zone

So much time has been taken to discuss physical surroundings as related to getting into the zone of studying. However, the physical and mental states are just as important, if not more so. Ensuring that you are staying physically and mentally healthy is essential to making sure that you are in the right zone to succeed in college. Most schools offer several eating opportunities for students through a cafeteria, on-campus restaurants, and grocery stores either located on-campus or in the surrounding area. Different people have different nutritional needs, so this book is not seeking to lecture readers on how to eat right. Doing so is your own responsibility. The one piece of dietary advice that will be provided is to speak with an expert or research on the Internet the most important nutritional habits to embrace; notably, what food groups need to be prioritized the most when establishing proper eating habits.

Everyone knows about the stereotypical "college diet" of affordable foods, notably Ramen noodles. Yes, this is certainly an academic staple, but consider that this is not a sustainable food. Sure, money is tight in college, without a doubt. However, it is worth doing your research to see what healthier options are out there without breaking the bank.

For instance, if you are not vegan, consider the cost of a pack of eggs. Many consider eggs to be an excellent source of protein, and are a staple breakfast item that can be prepared any number of ways, so it can be hard to grow tired of them. The cost of a pack of eggs can be as little as less than one dollar. Some bulk stores, such as Costco Wholesale, carry two dozen eggs for around $3 or $4. Buying other foods in bulk is a good way to get more food for less money, as cafeteria meals can add up quickly.

Another great way to stay nutritious without breaking the bank is sticking to water. Cutting out soda is an excellent way to pursue or maintain a healthy lifestyle, and is consistently more affordable. Some people purchase large packs of plastic water bottles in bulk to save money, while others have water filters to be able to consume tap water safely. Many water fountains even come with a filtered waterspout in order to allow people to refill their reusable bottles. Most restaurants serve water for free, or at a substantially reduced price. Your college most likely provides free water to students somewhere on campus; if so, purchasing a reusable bottle is both eco-friendly and saves a significant amount of money.

Water is great and all, but what about caffeine? Water is not the go-to "cram the night of the test" drink. Generally, most people are going to go for either energy drinks or coffee, each in their own respective forms and brands. First, it is worth noting that different body types are going to respond differently to varying quantities of caffeine. Some might grab one or two energy drinks to get them through, while another may be ultra-sensitive to half a cup of normal coffee. Gauging your sensitivity to caffeine is very important, as you could potentially be awake too little or too long if incorrect. While doing so, it is helpful to look at the nutritional facts to see exactly how much caffeine is in whatever you are drinking. If it is black coffee, you can find the nutritional facts online. Once you have determined your ideal caffeine amounts, find the healthiest form of this, trying to cut out excess sugar and guarana. Do the little research it would take to determine if there is a better alternative.

You may wonder what all the hype over coffee is if you haven't already discovered it for yourself. Believe it or not, something as seemingly simple as coffee comes in all sorts of different forms, flavors, and blends. One can purchase ground coffee or whole bean coffee. With whole bean coffee, people have a grinder that blends it into an even finer powder than pre-ground coffee. Should you find yourself enjoying the smell of coffee, whole bean coffee emits the scent and fills the room when ground. Most people make coffee in a traditional coffee maker, though there are other methods of brewing such as pour-over, French press, or even instant coffee. All of these methods taste quite different to the refined coffee drinker, and many people have their own preference.

Exploring this world is interesting and fairly affordable, as most of the methods listed above are notably cheaper than purchasing your coffee every day at the coffee house. Some even prefer espresso over normal drip coffee, as espresso is stronger, thicker, and has a richer flavor. Espresso is the base of cappuccinos, macchiatos, Americanos, Frappuccinos, and lattes that have become progressively more common. However, if you enjoy the flavor on its own without all of the steamed milk and sugar, you can prepare it plain, maybe adding cream and/or sugar as you would to a normal cup of coffee.

Believe it or not, many different cultures and nations around the world have their own varieties of coffee and espresso, specifying their own blends and techniques. The drinks mentioned above that can be purchased at most coffee houses and chains are Italian; but despite their undoubted success and intertwining into American culture, they do not represent the universal variety. For instance, Turkish coffee has a very thick and dark consistency that is overwhelming compared to the watery texture of typical "American" drip coffee. Cuban coffee is also very strong, but the base of Cuban coffee is espresso, coming with varying quantities of steamed milk and sugar. Most forms are deliberately so strong that it is culturally and traditionally served in small mugs with saucers underneath.

You may be wondering why there is such an extensive discussion over coffee in this portion, as it branches off from the topic of academia and college life. Everything goes back to the discussion earlier about taking the opportunity to learn about different cultures and lifestyles, as doing so helps you develop and find what you like and enjoy in your own life. College, more so than high school or any other time in life, is the first substantial opportunity to explore different areas and opportunities of life, and not only to find yourself and express that, but also find what works for you in pursuing success. It is worth noting after this extensive discussion on caffeine that it is indeed an addictive substance if not consumed in moderation. While addiction to caffeine doesn't often go beyond feeling sluggish and lethargic, and certainly does not compare to the dependency brought on by alcohol and hard drugs, it is not healthy for the heart to consume too much of it, or too frequently. Find a pattern that works for your health, your wallet, and your daily routine.

Maybe caffeine isn't for you. Perhaps being able to stay up extensively boils down to being able to go to bed early and set a healthier sleeping pattern than the average college student. If this is the case for you, and you have the discipline to be able to do so, then go for it! Many people insist that working out, having a healthy diet, and maintaining a consistent and healthy sleep pattern are far more valuable than drinking caffeine. However, many would argue that doing so does not help one stay awake on the night of a big test or an overwhelming paper. In the end, different people embrace different lifestyles, and no one person has exactly the right answer that will apply to everyone universally. As such, it is worth exploring every avenue and discovering what works best for you individually.

So much has been discussed about diet, but what of physical activity? How can the average college student find the time to work out or engage in cardio activity if that habit has not already been established in high school? Very simply, just as this book has emphasized the importance of developing at least some form of social activity, the same needs to be done for physical activity. Exercise is a literal necessity—an essential function—in order for the human body to function well. A great element of physical activity for someone who is not keen on it is one of the countless opportunities to combine socializing and exercise. Many sports require two or more people to play and open up the opportunity for positive dialogue and bonding. Friendly competition is a great way to become closer with somebody that you care about; and if that competition becomes progressively less friendly and more aggressive, it then becomes an opportunity to see that the individual may not be the best person to associate with.

Consider some of the extensive situations that encourage socialization: walking or running on a treadmill side by side, spotting one another on the bench press, competing in a game of tennis or racquetball, walking around the track or even just the campus, shooting hoops with a group, having a weekly group meet to play football or soccer, signing up for an "Ultimate Frisbee" league, or playing one of the many varieties of golf such as traditional "ball-and-stick" golf, disc golf, or even "FootGolf," which is played with a soccer ball. This is just a small sample of all of the different activities you can engage in. Just think of all of the creative games you and your friends played during recess as a kid, some of which may have even been introduced by your teachers in grade school.

At the bare minimum, striving to get at least 10,000 steps per day is a good baseline goal to set, as doing so causes a shift in perspective. Should this be a priority, you will likely find yourself taking advantage of standing instead of sitting, taking the long way to get to class, or maybe opting to climb the stairs instead of riding the elevator. If you reside on your school's campus, chances are that most students walk or ride something to get to school, such as a bicycle or a skateboard. Making the simple choice to leave a few minutes early and take the longer path is a good habit to get into, and you'd be surprised at how quickly the steps add up.

Author's Experience

As mentioned in another "Author's Experience" portion, my undergraduate college was located on the side of a hill. This meant that students had to climb up the hill from the dormitories, which were set at the base, in order to get to the main stretch of buildings at the top. This extensive path on top of the hill was known on-campus as "The Promenade." One of the great elements of The Promenade was that it was very scenic and well landscaped, especially during the spring and autumn seasons when the scenery would shift. Having this natural beauty gave my sister and me the mutually shared idea that this stretch of campus would make for a great environment for hide-and-seek. As we gauged our friends' potential interest, we were actually surprised to find out that a significant group of people wanted to join. On the first Saturday night it was planned, we managed to get about 15-20 people to show up, so we played a variation of hide-and-seek called "Sardines."

This "Sardines" game is essentially the inverse of hide-and-seek. Whereas the latter involves all but one person hiding in different spots, the former involves one designated person finding a hiding spot, then the remaining group goes out to find them. The tricky part of this game is that the "hider" has to find a spot large enough for the remaining group to squeeze in, yet small enough to still be a hiding spot. One-by-one, each member of the group finds the hider until there is only one "seeker" remaining. This ends the round, and the remaining "seeker" has to take a turn as the initial hider.

Engaging in this game on a large, scenic college campus proved to be so much fun, and surprisingly hysterical. I don't feel at liberty to disclose all of the comical antics that went on as a group of fifteen idiots crammed into the bushes in front of a building, as we would try to make one another laugh. This became intense and suspenseful as the remaining seeker or seekers would walk by the hiding spot, completely oblivious of our presence just under them.

Also to my sister's and my surprise, this group continued to meet every so often when the weather was clear, and everyone seemed to really enjoyed it. The group grew a little bit and managed to drag some people out of the dormitories that tended to otherwise be shut in. Occasionally, some people in passing seeing all of us playing would even ask to join, opening the opportunity to get to know more people at the school.

As fun of a game as this proved to be, we found it to be a weirdly great opportunity for light exercise as well. Since The Promenade was lengthy and was oriented longways, you would have to walk the length of it while searching for the hider/s. If you were the designated hider, you were only given one minute to hide, so it would involve running across the campus in order to find a good spot. Most of us did not have smartphones or smart watches at the time, as they were not common or affordable then, but there's no doubt that we would have reached all of our respective 10,000 daily steps from this alone.

I know that this probably sounds goofy and unappealing, and my advice is not necessarily to play this game in particular. Rather, try to find something that not only fosters a positive and constructive social atmosphere, but also encourages remaining physically active. It can be as simple as a game of football, soccer, basketball, etc. Combining exercise with group activities makes you all the more productive when factoring in your own personal commitment to physical activity and is even more time efficient.

Part II: Exceed Your Goals

By this point, you may be wondering why there has not been an explicit section about time management. After all, it is the title on the cover. Confusion and frustration would be an understandable reaction at this thought. However, as we continue together into the second portion, just remember that one cannot even think of time management if the many facets of life are not in order. The implied concept associated with time management is organization, so there is no way to properly hone in on the skill of time management if everything else in the background is chaotic.

Additionally, despite there not being one specific section discussing time management explicitly yet, there have been a few tips and tricks to increasing time efficiency thrown into various sections, so keep an eye out for these tips and do your best to apply the information to your own life and schedule.

The idea of formalizing your goals may elicit an eye roll, but the truth is that establishing a structured format for the things you want to achieve in your life makes achieving those things that much easier. When one clearly and explicitly establishes what needs to be done in a methodical way, breaking every component down step by step, the tasks at hand all of a sudden seem doable as opposed to daunting. After all, you cannot accomplish your goals if you do not know how to set them.

For instance, here is an example of the most basic collegiate goal that (presumably) every college student has: "I am going to earn my degree."

Okay, this is certainly an invaluable goal to prioritize. However, what comes to mind when you read this? Four years of classes, late nights cramming for tests, scrambling to find a working printer on campus minutes before a paper is due (yes, there are still professors who insist on physical paper over digital submissions), Ramen noodles every night for three weeks, drama with your roommate/s, and other things that could cause chaos. Plus, what kind of degree are you getting? Bachelor's? Master's? Associate's? Yes, the goal above is simple in structure, but daunting in its deceivingly grand scale.

Let us now try a different approach. Instead of an overly simplistic and non-specific statement, how does a formalized goal look? Below is just one of an infinite combination of new perspectives to take on:

"By December of this year, I will have completed the first semester of my college career, having passed all six of my classes, and successfully enrolling in at least five more general requirements for the next semester."

Yes, this goal is significantly longer, and may seem much more overwhelming, but do yourself a favor and read over it again. Break this down into each individual statement and dwell on the work and time that each entails. It is certainly less daunting and gargantuan than the thought of all the events that are contained within four of the most stressful years of your life! What it all comes down to is that the lack of generality in the formal goal keeps your imagination from running wild and subsequently short-circuiting.

The job and responsibility of this author, and this book as a whole, is to help make your college experience less terrifying and to break it down to show you that you do indeed have what it takes! You may have your doubts, and you may have had struggles leading up to this point, but you have the ability to make it and even to excel. In order to help you see that, this section will focus on the process of formalizing your goals, as well as the value and importance of doing so to make your life that much easier.

Chapter 5: S.M.A.R.T. Goals

Different people have different ways of setting goals that work better for their respective minds, and different fields of study will adopt different techniques and approaches. Organizations, and indeed entire industries, make efforts to universalize goals in order to both increase efficiency and promote consistency amongst all parties involved. However, there is one commonly cited goal format that is easy to understand and implement: this is the S.M.A.R.T. Goal format, also formatted less formally as "smart goals."

As you could probably assess, S.M.A.R.T. is an acronym that represents the formatting and structural criteria for goals. After going through the concepts and components of each of the five letters, some examples will be provided and discussed.

Firstly, the "S" represents "Specific." Just as was demonstrated in Part II's introduction, make sure to specify what is being done, as well as how it is going to be completed and accomplished. There are ways to communicate the main components of your goals in a compressed and simple process, and this will be discussed further along. Secondly, the "M" stands for "Measurable." This process involves quantifying your goal in order to make it tangible; or, in simpler terms, adding a numeric value to what is being done so that it becomes more concrete. This way, when the goal is being evaluated, progress can actually be measured and tracked.

Again, examples and techniques will be provided as this portion continues.

The acronym continues into the third letter, which is "A." The two words that are used interchangeably for this are "Attainable" and/or "Achievable." Exactly as these words suggest, this concept encourages the implementation of goals that the writer knows can be achieved and accomplished. This portion is more about the mindset of the goal-writer or those whom the goal is about (if composed by a third party), as it makes an effort to encourage the target individual/s by presenting steps that are more easily achieved than the larger goal. Taking it a step further, the S.M.A.R.T. system specifies EASILY attainable or achievable goals, emphasizing and promoting the practice of crafting goals that YOU as the writer know you can do. You have likely heard the phrase "no one knows you better than yourself," and it is absolutely true. Even if it takes some reflection and introspection to figure out, there is no better person to determine what can or cannot be done based on past successes and failures. For those who are crafting a goal for another individual, breaking it down for them and making them a very active part of the process is essential to their own success.

The fourth letter, "R," stands for "Realistic." Going along with the former "Achievable" component, this tries to reel the more enthusiastic goal-writers back a bit, pulling their feet back down to earth and making sure that the goal is realistically achievable and will not result in burnout. It can be easy to become excited and bite off more than you can chew, and becoming overwhelmed can very easily result in someone losing momentum or even giving up hope. The challenge of implementing both realism and attainability/achievability into a goal is that the writer has to deliberately underestimate their own abilities in order to ensure that they will be reached. As stated, coming examples will provide more insight on this challenge.

Finally, at the tail-end of the acronym sits an incredibly important part of the process. The bookending "T" stands for "Timely" or "Timeliness." Again, just as the word suggests, goals should include a timeframe in which completion can be expected. Think of this as a self-enforced deadline. While this factor is similar to the aforementioned "Measurable" in that it makes it so you can actually track and record progress on the goal, this is not meant to create pressure like a deadline set by a professor or a supervisor. What is nice about the timeliness of a goal is that it can be customized to take as little or as long as the writer deems necessary. However, remember the importance of keeping this "realistic" while considering and creating a timeframe.

That is a lot of information for an acronym that is supposed to make your life simpler! Implementing all five of these checklist items may seem like a difficult balance, or an overwhelming task. Not to worry! There are a few different approaches to take. Another nice component of this format is that you are encouraged to use some variety and creativity in the way that you craft a list of smart goals.

Before we go into creating these goals, let us break down the example provided in the introduction to Part II. In considering the goal of pursuing a college degree, we started out with the generic statement of "I am going to earn my degree." As was stated along with the example, this statement leaves a lot to be desired. Obviously not every college student enrolls as a freshman and knows exactly what field they plan on pursuing. Even for many of those who do, plans change as time goes on. Some may begin their course in a certain department, then get as far as an internship or field placement, only to discover that they are actually miserable in that work environment. Maybe they just cannot handle the high-stakes pressure, and need to find a more relaxing job. Others might find that sitting at a cubicle desk for eight hours a day drives them to madness, and they need a career that involves being active. In any event, smart goals can still be specific while not specifying a career.

Below is the example of the goal revised using the S.M.A.R.T. formatting:

"By December of this year, I will have completed the first semester of my college career, having passed all six of my classes, and successfully enrolling in at least five more general requirements for the next semester."

Yes, this is a long goal, far longer than the former. However, when you break it down, it incorporates every component of S.M.A.R.T., thus providing a clear path to accomplishing the goal. Firstly, the goal is specific in that it outlines exactly what will be done. Six classes will be completed during the first semester of college. Then, it goes on to specify that five more general requirements will be enrolled in by the end of the semester. That tiny little blurb says a lot in a little bit of time. The writer is communicating to themselves and any reader that they will have met with their advisor to determine the best courses to take in order to meet their general requirements, which are basic classes that every student has to take in order to earn their degree. This is an important specificity, as most colleges offer a variety of general courses to select from. For instance, if there is a requirement for an art class (also known as a "credit," especially when discussing generals), one may be allowed to select a drawing/sketching, painting, sculpting, or art history course. So, it is important to meet with an advisor in order to discuss what is out there. Thanks to the specific mentioning of this task, the writer is holding themselves to doing so prior to completing the semester.

However, there is a deliberate lack of specificity that was left out of the goal. Read over it again. Do any additional details come to mind that could be thrown in there? Immediately, the question that could have been raised after reading this may have been that of the definition of "passed." Sure, one can technically pass a class with a "D" grade in a general course. However, different departments have different rules on what is an acceptable grade. Some departments do not allow for a student to pass with anything below a "C." Some may not even allow passing with anything below a "B." Granted, it was acknowledged that this is the student's first semester of college, so they are taking generals. Even still, the importance of specificity remains clear and present.

How would this specificity be implemented into a S.M.A.R.T. goal? Essentially, in order to do so, the soon-to-be discussed elements of "Measurable," "Attainable," and "Realistic" have to work together with "Specific" in order to produce a sensible result. First, consider how you performed in high school. Were you a straight-A student, a procrastinator who bordered on flunking out throughout all four years, or somewhere in between? Does success in school come easily for you, or do you have a learning disability such as dyslexia that has made academia a constant struggle for you? Again, no one knows you as well as you know yourself. As a result, you should know that old habits do not (easily) die, and your habits will carry over into college, at least for the first few weeks or months. With that in mind, consider what the minimal level of success is for you. In fact, you should consider this your safety net.

For those who generally succeed in school, usually achieving "A's," a smart goal would likely be structured to incorporate something like this:

"…maintaining at least a 3.8 GPA."

For anyone who has a learning disability, an appropriate modification might include something like this:

"…maintaining at least a C-grade average, and meeting to see an on-campus tutor for at least one hour per week."

For a slacker, their academic performance may not be mentioned at all within the goal. Rather, they may want to turn their habits around, instead incorporating this into the S.M.A.R.T. goal:

"…turning in my homework on time for at least three assignments per week."

One might read this and feel like it is not ambitious enough. However, this is where the "Realistic" element becomes essential. Goals are there to help with progress, not solve problems immediately. In creating goals, remember that they are stepping stones toward change, and should be crafted periodically. Further into Part II, we will discuss the differences between short-term goals and long-term goals. For now, the examples provided are written with a short-term basis in mind.

Now, looking at the second letter, which is "M" for "Measurable," this goal can indeed be quantified. There were six classes this semester, and at least five more are being enrolled in for the coming semester, so it is easy to track the success of this goal. Despite the importance of further specificity being mentioned above in order to determine how passing is defined and determined, passing or failing is a concrete enough concept to make the results quantifiable and able to track easily. Additionally, measuring out the classes that were enrolled in for the coming semester can easily be done: were there five courses enrolled in? Yes? Okay, great, achieved! Again, remember that S.M.A.R.T. goals aim to make your success simpler and more achievable, not more overwhelming and complicated. As stated, these examples are short-term goals, breaking down long-term ambitions.

What are some other opportunities to implement a measurable element into a goal? One very common one may come to mind when considering life after college: income. Depending on the profession pursued, the regional cost of living, the state of the economy, etc., people often have a desired income in mind. Some look to just get by, some look to live comfortably, and others look to flourish. A single young adult might desire an annual income of "at least $65,000," as they are unmarried and do not have children. Depending on their field of study, this may or may not be a realistic salary coming out of college. Nevertheless, adding the phrase "at least" prior to the proposed income forms the aforementioned safety net, establishing that more may be earned annually, but this is the realistic minimum that can and should be earned.

Just as an income goal focuses on what is trying to be earned, measurable factors in goals can also account for what is trying to be avoided. For example: if someone has a temper and tends to drive aggressively, they may find themselves with multiple speeding tickets that have accrued. As a result, they might establish a smart goal to help reduce the number of tickets that they earn, incorporating a measurable element. For example: "...being issued no more than three speeding tickets this coming year." Depending on the circumstances and desired outcome, whether trying to avoid or enhance certain behaviors will determine the formatting and content of your measurability.

Just as it is important to make sure your measurability has a safety net, the same can be said of the applicable importance for "Achievability" and/or "Attainability." As stated before, this facet of goal-crafting involves making sure that you are indeed able to achieve what you set out to do. Should you construct an unreasonable or overly-ambitious goal, not achieving it will certainly be discouraging and set you off course. As such, the concept of a safety net or underestimating your abilities is vital to the success and satisfaction of the goal. Additionally, we never know what life holds in store, and we are never sure what circumstances and life events will get in the way of excelling. What if a family member passes away and the time dedicated to your goal is suddenly reduced? What if the job you've fought so hard for is taken away from you, and suddenly there is a substantial drop in income? Making sure that you are guaranteeing your success is vital to the achievability of the goal. After all, it comes back to the fact that no one knows you better than yourself, so who better to judge your own abilities than you?

What does this achievability or attainability look like within a goal? How do you make sure that what you are setting out to do is not overly ambitious and unreasonable? For the sake of this book being about college, as well as trying to be consistent, let us see how this played a part in the ongoing example:

"By December of this year, I will have completed the first semester of my college career, having passed all six of my classes, and successfully enrolling in at least five more general requirements for the next semester."

Breaking it down point-by-point, this student plans on finishing the semester by December. In American colleges, December is traditionally the end of each school year's first semester, issuing the beginning of Christmas break, just prior to returning in January for the next semester following New Year's. Some colleges work on a trimester system, and some spread the school year out even more. For the sake of this example, it will be assumed that this student's school works on a semester system. In this case, December is a perfectly reasonable time to expect to be done with the semester.

Next, it appears as if this student expects to have completed six classes within this time period. Not only that, but they then want to enroll in five more for the Winter/Spring semester. What is not specified in this scenario is how many credits each class is. The typical full college course is three credits. Shorter or lighter courses will account for one or two credits each, and a more intense course might be worth four credits if it requires laboratories or class time in addition to the main session. However, most courses above three credits do not come about until you have chosen your major area of study. It is not uncommon for many generals to only be worth one or two credits, so taking six classes might mean that four are full-credit (3 credits) and two are small electives (1-2 credits), adding up to between 14 and 16 credits. This is a busy semester, as one has to be working toward at least twelve credits per semester in order to be considered full-time. If this student is indeed enrolled in six full credit courses, that would mean they would earn 18 credits. This might not be the best idea for someone's first semester of college, but again, everyone should know their limit. While difficult for some, many students would find this very easy, especially if they are only taking general courses.

Finally, and very simply, there is the portion of the goal which mentions that the student will be enrolled in the next set of classes for the following semester by the end of the current one. In the modern era, class enrollment is completed online and can be done alone. Additionally, student advisors are available for appointments to assist students with signing up for classes. Setting up a time to review the degree audit and determine what is needed should not take an excessive amount of time, and very much ought to be done prior to finishing the current semester, as most schools have a designated time for enrollment. Although this is realistic and attainable for most students, the finances of college can throw a wrench into the wheel. Unfortunately, unpaid bills (out-of-pocket or from loans) result in students being placed on academic holds, which means that they are unable to sign up for classes until the balance has been resolved. If you find yourself in this position, meet with an academic advisor as soon as possible in order to determine the best course of action to take. Part of their job is to assist students with looking into different options available to them. Take advantage of this service and let them help you.

The elements of "Realistic" and "Achievable/Attainable" can easily blend together. In order to distinguish between the two, consider the latter to be more focused on "what can I do?", versus the former being more about "what is physically and/or mentally possible?" Realism in a goal is more about objective possibility. For instance, as just discussed, the decision whether or not to take four, five, six, or seven courses in a semester is very different than someone trying to do four years' worth of college in three semesters. Doing so would be objectively impossible for most students, and for those who could, their mental health and even academic success would both be pushed to their respective limits. Although not commonly used, you can use the synonym of "Reasonable" to put this one into perspective. Instead of "Can you do it?" shift more toward, "Can ANYONE do this?"

"Timeliness" is the last of the five factors to consider in this system. Obviously, this component deals with the question of how long the goal will take. However, very much like the importance of measuring, the goal has to be able to be tangibly tracked, holding the goal-setter accountable for completing the task by a specific, non-arbitrary time. In looking at the ongoing example, the student is looking to finish their first semester of college by December. As discussed, this is realistic and attainable because the average American first semester ends in December. Also, the lack of specificity of a date may seem like it is breaking the first rule in the S.M.A.R.T. system. However, the month is specific enough in this case, as the end of a semester can be delayed for any number of reasons. Also, there are plenty of cases where a final exam or final paper may be delayed, putting the end of the semester off. This is also why it may not be the best idea to document an end-date or end-month for your expected graduation. Family emergencies, school emergencies, and other unexpected events are going to come up without any notice. One can say that they are prepared for anything, physically or mentally, but there is no way to know for sure until something actually occurs.

For instance, how many of us felt prepared in any way for the COVID-19 pandemic? The world stopped turning, and so many students who had worked through blood, sweat, and tears to get to graduation had to shelve their caps and gowns. Think about when the pandemic hit the United States: February and March 2020. How convenient that this had to be just before spring, when so many people graduate in the months of May and June. Eventually, the world learned to adjust and there were graduation ceremonies over webcam, but how disappointing must it have felt to not get to walk across a stage? Even worse, how many people had to wait months to finish what was left of their schooling when everything shut down? There was no way of being prepared for any of this, especially for young students, and everyone had to find their own ways of adjusting.

Part of the secret to smart goals is that they are not meant to be stretched out over enormous amounts of time. Just as the thought of the unrevised goal of "I am going to earn my degree" is overwhelmingly stretched out over years at a time, the formal goal covers one semester of the typical eight semesters that a college career entails. One-eighth is certainly more manageable and is an undoubtedly more realistic timeframe than four years. With that said, and with the idea of smart goals in mind, let us consider the differences between short-term goals and long-term goals in the coming chapter.

Chapter 6:
Short- and Long-Term Goals

As stated, the recurring examples have been examples of short-term goals. The surface level difference between a long- and short-term goal is the expected timeframe in order to reach completion. With a typical short-term goal, it may take anywhere between a few days and a few months, rarely lasting any more than six months or so. This is not so much a rule as a typical expectation. Any longer than this is expected to be more of a long-term goal, which can last years. Despite long-term goals lasting far longer, they are not so much seen as life goals. Rather, they are supposed to be points that need to be addressed, but are not expected to last ten years. A long-term goal may continue to be re-established if it is not accomplished, which is especially relevant in cases of behavioral intervention.

A common example of such a recurring case is that of substance abuse. The long-term goal for someone struggling with addiction would involve both achieving and maintaining sobriety. For those who do not know much about the recovery process, an established structure known by some as the "Cycle of Recovery" was created to account for the likelihood of relapse, which is when an individual uses their substance of choice again. Even if it is an isolated incident, and even if it follows complete and loyal sobriety for 15 years, it is still perceived as a relapse, causing the individual to start the recovery process all over again. In such cases, a long-term goal remains active, as it starts right back from the beginning.

Outside of special cases like this, which are certainly worth acknowledging, long-term goals are usually reduced down to a few years. However, the differences between short-term goals and long-term goals go so far beyond simply the time that they each take to accomplish. If that were the case, they would exist independently of each other. Rather, short- and long-term goals interact together and generally cannot, and should not, exist without the other. The purpose of a short-term goal is to break down the overall long-term goal into S.M.A.R.T. steps to help the individual pursue what needs to be accomplished.

With the recurring short-term example of getting through the first semester of college, the long-term goal was actually listed in Part II's introduction: "I am going to earn my college degree." Despite this being a fairly lazily formatted long-term goal, it is a stereotypical long-term goal, nevertheless. For the sake of proper goal setting, let's reformat this into a more proper long-term goal, utilizing the S.M.A.R.T. method, before we continue:

"Within the next five years, I will earn one bachelor's degree in psychology with a GPA of at least 3.1."

This goal specifies the type of degree being earned and the desired GPA. It is measurable by providing the number of degrees desired, as some people desire to graduate as a double-major with two bachelor's degrees, as well as specifying a specific GPA that is desired. By phrasing the goal to say "…a GPA of at least 3.1," it is presumed to be an easy GPA for the goal's writer to achieve. The goal is realistic in that most college students graduate in about four years, so it adds an extra year to account for any extenuating circumstances that may prolong the completion of college. This five-year period also fulfills the timely component, specifying a measurable time period to complete everything in. It is worth noting that the goal says, "five years," not "five school years" or "ten semesters," so it allows for summer or winter courses if need be.

With all of that out of the way, let's get back to the discussion of long- and short-term goals. When comparing this new long-term goal with the recurring example of the short-term first semester goal, it is clear that the two are intertwined with each other. They both discuss the completion of a collegiate milestone, as well as the expected time of completion. The problem with long-term goals that many people fall into is that they abandon the S.M.A.R.T. format and resort to oversimplified phrases, such as in the above example.

Why is it that this format is abandoned with long-term goals? Very simply, and actually understandably, some see smart goals as only short-term because the system allows, and even encourages, flexibility for change and growth. As such, it probably seems to many that smart goals cannot be concrete and established. Despite this thought making sense, it is not remotely the case. A long-term goal MUST feel just as accomplishable as a short-term goal, and not adding any of the criteria, but especially specificity, is just going to make the goal seem overwhelming and undoable. Even if the long-term goal is traditionally left unaltered, it should be just as encouraging and motivational as the short-term goal.

In this case, how can long-term goals be crafted from generic, blank statements to smart goals? Let us use an example for something outside of completing college. Keeping it practical and relatable, we will look at how a long-term goal might look within the context of something more recreational:

"I want to find someone to date."

Hopefully, some red flags go up when you read this, mainly that this does not appear as a goal at all! Goals are certainly a reflection of what is desired, though they are not phrased as simply what you want. A more goal-oriented version of this statement would be the following:

"I will begin dating someone."

Okay, so we will try and form this into a smart goal. First, approaching the subject of dating is difficult because different cultures and lifestyles use different terminology. Some might hear the term "dating" and think that it refers to casually going out with different people, some might think of casually going out with one person, and still others might think that it indicates an actual relationship. With that in mind, we will implement some specificity, the first "S" in "smart":

"I will establish a dating relationship with a girl."

Now that the intention of the goal-setter is a little more clearly defined, both the nature of the relationship and the desired gender, we progress to the next letter of "M", or "measurability." This may seem unnecessary, as most would read the goal above and assume that the person wants a relationship with one person. However, it is still important to establish and specify how many relationships one wants to be in. An individual might desire a scenario where they engage in multiple relationships over a particular time period, perhaps to develop their dating experience a little more and learn more about who and what they are looking for. Even in the moments when it seems unnecessary to implement one of the S.M.A.R.T. components, it is still important to do so. With that said, let's add a measurable variable to this:

"I will establish one dating relationship with a girl."

Next is the facet of "attainability" or "achievability." For some, entering into a dating relationship comes very easily, as they meet a lot of new people and feel more natural when asking someone out. Maybe they already go out on so many dates on a regular basis that it is only a matter of opting to settle down. In these cases, setting a goal may need to be more focused on how long the relationship should last, turning the one above into a short-term goal. For others, their experience is the complete opposite. The nerves when simply approaching someone attractive consume and prevent any success with initiating a date. For these individuals, the short-term goals need to be centered around taking baby steps toward developing the social skills needed to find a relationship. Additionally, it may be best to embrace a long-term goal of going on a certain number of dates instead of establishing a relationship. Such an individual could also potentially extend the timeliness of this long-term goal, but we will come to that.

For the sake of this example, let us assume that the goal-setter is somewhere in-between, and assume that this is a feasible yet somewhat intimidating goal. After all, no one can predict where life will take them, whether closer to a relationship or further away from any prospects. In this case, the current goal is more realistic remaining a long-term goal, though a little more specificity can make it more attainable:

"I will establish and maintain one dating relationship with a girl, increasing frequency of socialization as needed to meet new people."

This is a little lengthier, but accounts for the need to take action if the means being taken are not working. Hopefully, adding this little bit may also remove some of the pressure of scrambling to find a relationship. If someone is too desperate to get into a relationship, as opposed to finding the right person and allowing the relationship to occur naturally, there will be little opportunity for growth and maintenance of a long-term setup. It may also be worth adding another long-term goal over a more expansive amount of time to address the desire (or lack thereof) for an eventual marital relationship, but let's not get too far ahead of ourselves.

Is this a realistic goal? Can most people find a relationship? Yes, it is the belief and conviction of this author that it is very much safe to assume that most people are able to find and engage in a dating relationship. Whether or not the arrangement will last is another factor entirely, though the idea of engaging in a relationship is indeed realistic. Even for those who struggle to socialize in general, not even just with the groups whom they are sexually attracted to, two people who are less socially oriented are able to come together, even if their mutual experience is the social struggle itself.

The one remaining factor that will certainly determine the realism and attainability/achievability of this goal is that of "timeliness." How possible is it for someone to establish this goal, then run out the door and snag a relationship in a day? A week? A month? A year? Believe it or not, this question actually goes back to the current state of your social life. How often do you go out and socialize with your friends? How many dates do you go on? Along with that, how many potential candidates for a relationship are you currently in contact with? Are there any that you are currently speaking with or seeing regularly? So many factors play a part in this, which goes back to the former point that no one knows you better than yourself. If you are being honest with yourself, no one should intervene and tell you that you are incorrect.

With all of this in mind, let's look at our hypothetical goal-setter again. He feels confident in his ability to pursue a girlfriend, though he is still somewhat intimidated by the idea of putting himself out there to the degree that is needed in order to establish that intimate of a relationship. As a result, he sits down and considers how many dates he has been on in the years leading up to this goal. Without thinking too hard about it, he estimates that he went on about four dates in the past year, though each one was with a different girl. Nothing really panned out due to mutual disinterest, and he was usually fine with this.

Going out on Friday and Saturday nights was pretty common, though it was pretty rare for him and his friends to go to a bar or a club. Socializing would usually involve going to the same coffee house and either talking or playing board games. Occasionally, they would meet up for a party, though it would usually be a fairly quiet affair with the same people. Now that he has graduated from high school and is a freshman in college, just starting out in his first semester, he has started to attend a campus of roughly 25,000 students. The ratio of men to women is about 1:1, or 50%, so there is a fair number of people out there for him to meet, especially since he is residing in the dormitory on campus.

With these factors in mind, he has also been feeling somewhat down and depressed, mainly lonely in this new place, as all of his close friends either went to different schools or found jobs instead of going to college. The idea of having a girlfriend has been somewhat comforting, and he has felt a motivation to find someone after not being particularly interested in relationships in high school. Due to this current, positive drive that he has been experiencing, along with the immediate need to meet new people, he figures that he will certainly make new friends while pursuing a dating relationship.

After processing all of this information, he finally decides that giving himself one calendar year would be plenty of time to find someone. An entire twelve months even felt a bit long, as he wanted to get out there as soon as possible. Though he started to write this down into his notebook, the pen stopped scribbling. He dwelt on this further, and remembered that he would not be on the school's campus for a full calendar year, as he would move back home once the second semester was over. Additionally, he would not be there during spring break or Christmas break, as well as some sporadic weekends throughout the school year, as he only lived about two and a half hours from home. Despite the inward confidence that he felt about his ability to find something meaningful, he felt it best to extend this goal to two years. This, he felt, needed to be more of a long-term goal in order to ensure that he did not rush into anything.

Sure enough, toward the end of the second semester, he met an amazing girl, someone so far beyond what he had initially hoped for. Although their relationship did not begin right away, they continued to talk over the phone during summer break, as she lived on the other side of the country. He even went out to visit her for a few days. Once they got back to school for the next year, he asked her to be his girlfriend and she happily agreed. When he looked back on the goal, he figured out that it did indeed take a little over a year, though only by a few weeks. Along the way, he also managed to make an amazing set of friends, both men and women, and he has been pleasantly surprised at how quickly everyone has grown so close.

This is the final goal that ended up in his notebook:

"I will establish and maintain one dating relationship with a girl, increasing frequency of socialization as needed to meet new people at least once per month, and will do so in no more than two calendar years."

Thankfully, this hypothetical story ended happily. Our hero took the time to establish a Specific, Measurable, Attainable/Achievable, Realistic, and Timely long-term goal.

What do you think would have happened had he not met this amazing girl and reached his proposed timeframe of one year? He likely would have felt some level of discouragement and/or frustration. However, as a result of having given himself more time, he was able to keep moving forward.

As you will read in the coming "Author's Experience," the better short-term goals are spread out over six months. As such, a long-term goal ought to be longer than six months. Even if you predict that it will only take you a few months at most to find a significant other, remember that a good goal always has a safety net, regardless of whether it is on a short- or long-term basis. If you expect to find a relationship in a month, allow yourself three months in the goal. If you think it will take a year, give yourself two years. Always account for life's unpredictability and the factors that are completely out of our control.

Author's Experience

As was stated before, I obtained my bachelor's degree in psychology. After college, I decided to pursue a master's degree in social work instead of psychology due to it allowing for more of a general degree and less sectioned into specialties, amongst many other factors that I refuse to bore you with. Having had classes in two mental health fields, I had the S.M.A.R.T. goal system drilled into my memory.

The first job that I took on right out of college was that of a case manager, which I continued through my master's program. Essentially, a case manager is a social worker who helps adults with mental health diagnoses and Medicaid (state insurance) pursue independence in society. For the child program, the assistance provided was centered more around behavior and development, as well as promoting healthy family and peer relationships.

The particular company that I worked for made claims about "putting the client first," as well as taking care of their employees. As I quickly found out, neither of these were remotely true, and they turned out to be absorbed with profitability and quick expansion instead of developing what they currently had. Subsequently, they overworked their employees, and developed an average turnover rate (the amount of time most people either quit or are terminated) of two to three months.

I worked for this company for three and a half years. Since I was unmarried without children, and was the youngest employee at my branch for a long time, I was asked to assume many different roles over the years that required extra time and involvement. One of the last roles that I took on (while also maintaining my previous responsibilities) was to become the branch's intake specialist. This position meant that I would complete every intake for new clients, as well as the required six-month reassessments that were needed to keep current clients active in the company.

Both of these types of meetings were very involved and very detailed. Releases of Information (allowing communication between case managers/company staff and various organizations involved with the client) had to be signed or updated, all of the client's mental health, somatic (physical) health, family history, and social history had to be recorded for intakes, or reviewed and updated for reassessments, and consent forms had to be reviewed and signed by hand. Nothing was electronic for these meetings and they required an overwhelming amount of work for both the intake staff and the already fragile clientele involved. One of the most important parts of these meetings was the development or revision of care plans, which are a collection of goals for each client. There were three types of goals in these care plans: overall goals, and then long-term and short-term goals within each individual goal. The "overall goals" did not have a formal term and were usually just referred to simply as "goals." An example of a typical care plan would be a collection of mental health, socialization, occupational, and compliance (with case manager appointments) goals.

Due to the organization not practicing what they preached and micromanaging the efficiency of their workers, the care plans were often overlooked, and intake staff often took shortcuts and created oversimplified, templated goals instead of implementing the S.M.A.R.T. system. As I began to reassess people in the program, I was shocked to find that a mental health goal's long-term objective would simply say, for example, "John will achieve mental health." Then, the short-term goal would simply say, "John will attend therapy." This was shocking, especially considering that these were submitted to insurance companies. How embarrassing!

As I assumed this role, I began to speak with the clients to get them involved in the formation and revision of these documents. After all, the care plan was a formal document that required their signature, yet they were not even aware of the goals that they were formally agreeing to! In starting to get

77

them involved, as well as implementing the S.M.A.R.T. goals system, the clients began to both visually and verbally express a sense of hope and motivation. Suddenly, the generic "John will achieve mental health" turned into, "John will maintain mental health stability, reducing spells of anxiety (or whatever symptom/s their condition/s would cause) down to no more than once per week." Then, the short-term goal would look something like this: "John will attend and engage in at least two appointments with his therapist per month." Simple, yes; but many times the client would say, "But I go once a week." I would then tell them, "That's great! Then you're already accomplishing the goal! We just need to make sure it doesn't slip under that number." This would frequently make them light up, especially if they were hard on themselves and felt like they had been failing at other facets of life. What is a better way to boost someone's motivation and help give them a nudge, instead of bogging them down with the overwhelming, confusing, and arbitrary goals that preceded these? Plus, how much more encouraging is it to be able to give someone the hope that they can work to reduce the burdens that come about as a result of their mental health conditions? Seeing some phrases like "…to reduce anxiety…" or "…to reduce depression…" was so healing for them, as these conditions felt eternal, like there was no hope to ever find relief from them.

This story may have been about creating goals for others, but think about how this would play out if you did this for yourself. As has been regurgitated throughout this section, arbitrary goals cause the imagination to run wild. Growing up in the culture that I did, it took me a long time to accept that there is nothing wrong with making life easier for yourself—physically, mentally, emotionally, spiritually, relationally, and other facets of your life. It is still an ongoing struggle, but using smart goals to help you along will certainly help you perceive the metaphorical glass as half-full, not half-empty.

Part III: Balance College Life

So much has been discussed of the college life as a whole, with all of the intricacies and many facets that it contains: socialization, academia, organization and cleanliness, professionalism and networking, etc. However, not much has been discussed in the way of time management. As was established, there is so much that has to be discussed first before even being able to approach the admittedly daunting subject of time management. After all, the other components of one's life need to be at least somewhat in order before being able to balance time. How can someone expect to be able to complete their homework at full efficiency if they live in a pigsty? If one is not organized, they might lose some important papers that are needed for a project. Similarly, if another person has not made the time to get out of their dorm room or apartment to socialize, and instead has remained as a recluse in order to focus and get various projects completed with the thought and spirit of being a dedicated student, they might go stir crazy and lose momentum, achieving burnout. As is the case in life, there is a delicate balance to everything, and being able to have a grip on life is important before expecting to be successful elsewhere. However, with everything that we have talked about so far, the time has come to finally begin exploring the titular subject of "time management" and how some of the basics of balancing time can be applied to your collegiate career.

Before jumping in, it is invaluable to resurrect the ongoing disclaimer that everything in this book should be personalized. It is impossible to craft advice without causing some people to roll their eyes and disregard it; but believe it or not, that is more than okay! In fact, that is a positive thing. By someone disregarding another's advice, it heavily implies that they have found a way that is better for them. In such cases, they have already personalized their own methods and made it work for them and their own systems of development. Sure, there are plenty of arrogant people out there that are delusional and think they have all the answers. This does not apply to such people, as the chances of such individuals even picking up a book that gives advice are pretty low.

What even is "time management?" Can it be defined as a concept for the sake of exploring what it is? In the first chapter of this third section, we will explore the importance of first establishing what is important to you as a college student.

Chapter 7: Core Values

Within the sciences, there is a term and concept known as "operational definition." This is used to define something as it applies specifically to a study, experiment, journal entry, etc. In other words, it is a definition that does not try to define something in general as a whole. Rather, it seeks to define something ONLY as it applies to the piece being written or the data being recorded. Think of this as a game of Monopoly that you and your family or friends play regularly. Many households customize the game with their own twists and rules. As a result, when other people come over to play, they have their own expectations of how the game ought to be played and how the rules ought to be applied. This conflict can result in long-winded arguments and getting the rule book back out. How much easier would it be to simply establish these customized rules from the start? This is where operational definitions come into play.

Now that this has been established, the term "time management" will be operationally defined as "the ability for one to balance multiple responsibilities, both formal and informal, demonstrating the ability to provide the needed time to each whilst not neglecting any facet."

Let us break this down together, as there was quite a bit of information crammed into that small section. Firstly, "the ability for one to balance multiple responsibilities." Suddenly, the importance of the first two parts becomes more evident! While this book may be specific to collegiate life, think of all of the different careers and lifestyles out there. It can be difficult to write a definition that takes all of these into consideration, so making sure to use generalities is important. Have you ever been to a big city? New York? Chicago? Los Angeles? Have you had the opportunity to walk on the sidewalk, seeing all of the different people scurrying around? It is absolutely overwhelming, almost magical in a strange way. Some walk, some take the bus, some take the train system, some bike, some hitch a taxi, and some drive. In all of these settings, it seems as if no two people are going to the same place. Everyone has their priorities, their tasks, their lives. No two lives are exactly the same, despite all of the similarities that bring us together. As such, no one can tell you how to live your life and prioritize your values except you. This is why your ability to figure out your own method of time management is so important to discover and develop.

Next, the operational definition continues by adding, "both formal and informal." Certainly, this book has explored both social and academic components, discussing the importance of each. However, as your life continues, the lines between formal and informal responsibilities starts to become a little blurred. What is desirable and what is necessary are suddenly not as clear-cut as they seemed in the past. Unfortunately, this is a natural part of growing up. Within this chapter, we will take a look at one of the theories about decision-making that came from a very famous man in the field of psychology.

Finally, the last portion of the definition states that time management is achieved when someone is "demonstrating the ability to provide the needed time to each whilst not neglecting any facet." Just as it states, being able to balance everything while not neglecting another component of your life is the truest sense of time management. We are all given time, some more than others, and our ability to disperse it where it needs to be spread is essential. There is nothing wrong with saying that something needs to be addressed at a later time. In fact, this is a big part of proper time management, and will be discussed later in Part III. However, an individual has achieved a proper sense of time management when that "later" point arrives, and they are indeed able to address what was initially put off. Sometimes, unpleasant things need to be addressed, and someone who has matured with a sense of time management will be better prepared to allot the time needed to get it done.

With this operational definition of "time management" established, what immediately comes to your mind? How does it apply to you? Are there any particular memories or associations to your own life and experiences coming up? It is the hope of this author that they are, as whatever associations are resurrected in your mind are going to play a big part in your ability to prioritize what parts of your life are more or less important to allot time to.

As promised, let us look at a very famous psychological model that examines the way in which we make decisions. In the late 19th century, Dr. Sigmund Freud proposed the "Psychoanalytic Theory," which includes three terms that you may have heard over the years: "Id," "Ego," and "Super-Ego." Freud created these three terms in his theory to represent three states of the subconscious, specifically centered around our process of decision-making.

First, the "Id" represents the ultimate selfish, primal, and juvenile parts of our brain. The Id is the little boy screaming at the grocery store over his mother not buying him candy. "I WANT CANDY! I DESERVE IT! CANDY TASTES GOOD! I DESERVE TO TASTE CANDY AND BE HAPPY!" It is an inherently selfish part of the brain. This is, in a deconstructed way, how the Id thinks. Children do not have developed Egos or Super-Egos, so it makes sense to think of them as problematically selfish. What more appropriate insult is there for someone who is acting self-centered than to call them "childish"?

Next, the "Super-Ego" is the portion of the decision-making subconscious that is the complete polar opposite of the Id. Instead of being self-centered and self-pleasing, it is the portion of the model that deals with morality and wisdom, prioritizing "the right thing" over what is naturally more desirable, putting the self aside. It is the mother who gives her child the last bit of food that is in the cupboard, or the person who gives all of their spare time to charity. Its language would consist of phrases such as, "Give them your seat. Your vision is good enough to see from the back" or "It doesn't matter if you're running late; that elderly woman over there is struggling to carry her grocery bags, so go help her." Essentially, the Super-Ego is the altruistic part of our decision-making, as altruism is defined as the ultimate level of selflessness, especially when there is no incentive to doing the moral or selfless deed.

As you can probably imagine, this Id and Super-Ego are mortal enemies, often fighting to be the dominant decision-maker. However, as is the case with every organized fight, there has to be a moderator. This is where the "Ego" comes into play. The Ego takes the arguments from both sides and tries to compromise between the two. According to Freud's theory, part of maturing is the development of the Ego and the decision-making process to be progressively less self-centered. Nevertheless, the Id is still an important part of the decision-making process, as it helps us look after our own needs.

A very common example of this model as a whole in practice is how it applies to human sexuality. Urges are common in both men and women, especially in college. However, what is done about these urges is very important, and can be demonstrated in the following model:

One morning, around 9:00 AM, a man has a strong desire to engage in sexual intercourse. His Id communicates that "sex will be obtained before lunch today." The Super-Ego intercedes and states that this may not be feasible, as a meeting is scheduled from 10:00 AM - 1:30 PM. The Id responds by suggesting that the man run home and have sex with his wife. The Super-Ego responds by stating that it would be dishonest to leave the office while on the clock, as there is quite a bit of work to do anyway. Plus, the man took the train into work, and getting home and back before 10:00 AM would be virtually impossible. On top of that, his wife may not even be in the mood to have sex. The Id then proposes that the man try to have sex with one of the women at the office, maybe the cute secretary that replaced his now-retired former assistant. The Super-Ego speaks up and states that it would be wrong for the man to cheat on his wife. Additionally, doing so would be an abuse of his status, and would disrespect any relationship that another woman might be in. The battle continues until the Ego takes points from each side and reaches a decision, leading the man to decide to call his wife and see if she would be interested in having sex after the meeting is over. If not, he will take care of his urge independently at a later time.

Yes, this example is bizarre, intense, and somewhat gruesome to think about. However, it is a realistic depiction as to how some people think. What was not disclosed prior to the example is that this man struggles with a diagnosed sex addiction which, believe it or not, is a real mental health condition. As such, satisfying his high libido (a.k.a. sex drive) is a very high priority for him, and his mind is on it. It is also worth noting that just because his Ego reached that conclusion at 9:02 AM, it does not mean that the battle was over for him. During his 10-1:30 meeting, he found himself distracted during the whole meeting. He caught his eyes drifting through the glass walls of the conference room to his secretary's desk, and the temptation only continued. We can only hope that this man made the right decision, though unfortunately many do not. Impulse control can be hard, especially when you do not have a grounded and firmly established system of values.

Becoming a college student is a big deal, and it is certainly a peek into complete, independent adulthood. For many, it is the absolute first time that they are independent of their parents. As such, making sure to develop maturity in decision-making is absolutely essential. Much of this book has discussed the importance of balancing socialization, or in this case, desired activities, and that of the responsibility of work and academia. However, both of these variables are pretty vague until you individualize one's priorities. To some, the time needed to play video games takes precedence over time with family. For others, making the time to study for a weekly quiz is more essential than going out to eat with a group of friends.

What everything comes down to is the basic concept of establishing a system of values in oneself. What are the things that are most important to you? If given a choice between allotting time to one of two things, which of the two will always take priority? Are there exceptions to that rule? Are your needs always more important than the needs of those around you? Do you have any religious views, and if so, do they require any of your time and attention? Do you pray to anyone or anything? These are only some of the basic questions that you want to ask yourself when deciding what is important to you. However, unlike the tangibility of smart goals, establishing a set of values is not as prevalent in writing as it is in practice.

What does this mean? How can values be practiced and established simultaneously? Actually, this is very simple: you will naturally allot time to the things that are most important to you. At its core, this is the most important factor when considering how to succeed in time management. Managing time is not always as simple as allotting a few hours to this, or a few minutes to that. Rather, it is the ability for someone to focus and allot the amount of time that is NEEDED in order to complete something correctly and successfully. The most obvious example that can be related to college life is that of studying. Deciding to allot three and a half hours to study for a final exam is not particularly helpful if the student has struggled in this class throughout the semester. It is much more valuable for the student to establish that they will put in the time needed to study for that exam, no matter how long it takes.

Wait a second, what happened to all of this about balancing your time and priorities? What happened to the ability to balance everything in life? What happened to the skill of allotting time to work on multiple things? Yes, the thought of devoting one entire evening to one task seems unproductive and overwhelming. There is so much to be done in the life of a college student, and seemingly so little time to do it. Does the student have to give any time to cleaning their living space? Is there any laundry to catch up on? What about any job that this student has? How are they going to stay fed and hydrated while staring at a book? Will an entire evening burn the student out for the rest of the week?

Let us take a look at how this evening turned out. The student went to her two classes from 8:00 AM - 11:30 AM, then walked to the nearby grocery store for her 12:00 PM -5:00 PM shift. While at the store, she bought a meal from the hot bar and a small pint of ice cream as a study snack and an incentive to focus on her studies. She has a reusable water bottle with a filter back at her dorm room, so she usually does not have to purchase water bottles and has all of her drinks covered. After making the trip by foot back to her dormitory, she checked her smart watch and found that she was at 7,400 steps for the day. This was admittedly frustrating for her, considering that she would usually be at 9,500 by this time of day. Considering she would be sitting down for most of the rest of the day, she dropped her food and ice cream off into her mini fridge and went back outside to get a little closer to her desired step count.

Taking another 25 minutes for a quick speed-walk proved to be a wise choice, as it lifted her step count to a more reasonable 8,600. This was not quite what she would like, but a jump of 1,200 made her feel better about sitting. Additionally, doing so gave her the chance to listen to her designated "pumped" playlist, shifting her into the mindset to focus. Once back in the room, she switched the music over to her room speaker, changing to her study lo-fi playlist. The sun was still high, despite it already being 6:15 in the evening, so she made sure to open her blinds and crack the window to let some of the summer air in. To accompany the soothing rhythms of her music, she lit the three wicks of her favorite scented candle and turned off the sink light that her roommate had left on while running out. Thankfully, this scattered roommate had not returned for the evening yet, so she would still have some peace and quiet to focus.

With the mind and the mood both set, she unzipped her backpack and produced her laptop and textbook. She never considered herself obsessive or "type-A" by any means, though she was the first to admit that she was very particular with the way in which she took her lecture notes on the computer and stored them on her desktop. This organization paid off on evenings like this. Once loaded up and on the charger, she opened the file with her school's name. From there, the path to her notes was Year III > Semester II (Winter) > Organic Chemistry II (CEM 252), and each document of class notes was titled with the date of the lecture.

As her professor did not believe in comprehensive examinations, she was able to identify the last eight lectures and began to review her notes.

Before she even had a chance to realize it, two hours had flown by, as her smart watch now read 8:23 PM. Thanks to her ability to get into the zone, she had used those two hours extremely efficiently, having reviewed four of the eight lectures in depth. However, she still had not eaten, and it was actually her stomach growling that had pulled her from her mental zone. Finishing up the last bit of the fourth set of notes, she took her dirty clothes hamper and went to the laundry room down the hall, throwing in a load of darks set to "Quick Run." None of the other machines were in use tonight, so she knew that she would have some time to spare without running the risk of someone throwing her clothes on the floor to make room.

Coming back to her room, she produced the hot meal that she had purchased for dinner and put it in the microwave for the recommended four minutes. After punching "Start," she took a quick bathroom break and washed her hands thoroughly, then grabbed her pre-filled water bottle from the fridge. By this point, the food was done, and she put on an episode of her favorite sitcom to watch while she ate. This is a show that she had seen countless times through, and hardly had to pay attention, even hardly laughed, while mentally reciting the lines in-between bites. Like clockwork, the 22-minute runtime episode ended just as she was taking the last few chews of her meal. Immediately after disposing of the Styrofoam box and plastic silverware that the food came in, she wiped her desk down with a disinfectant wipe. It was no sooner than the wipe went into the garbage that she remembered her clothes in the washing machine, which sent her flying out the door. She was relieved to find that the other washing machines and dryers in the laundry room had remained unoccupied, but still did not hesitate to quickly fluff her clothes and transfer them to a dryer.

As her dorm room door drew nearer, she reached into the designated left pocket of her sweatpants, but her heart sank. In the hurry to return to the laundry room, she had neglected to remember the key that still remained on her key dish. Knocking on her suitemates' door proved fruitless, as she later remembered that both work late shifts at their respective jobs. Even her RA, who stayed just a few doors down, did not answer to her knocks.

Fuzzy socks and all, our heroine made the short yet irritating journey through the long yet familiar maze of doors, down the steps, and into the girls' dormitory library. Upon her arrival, the head RA was having a goofy conversation with the front desk worker. Even after approaching her and asking for help, the student was met with irritation from the head RA, who told her to wait until she was done with her conversation. The student patiently waited; but before she knew it, ten minutes had flown by! She could not believe it, nor the audacity of the RA to do this, so she politely interrupted the conversation and insisted that the RA help her now. Despite the huffs and eye rolls, the RA followed the determined student back up the stairs and through the corridors, opening her room back up for her.

Things were just as she had left them; candle burning, music playing, and computer still open. Without hesitation, she went right to her key dish and placed the reunited key card in her designated left pocket to prevent this fiasco from reoccurring. Once back at the computer, she initially struggled to get back into the zone after opening the notes for lecture five, so she reached into the freezer of her mini fridge and produced the small pint of ice cream, along with a spoon. The choice of the molten brownie flavor was no accident, as it had been her favorite flavor of ice cream since she was a little girl, even down to that particular brand. Memories of eating it on the first days of summer vacation did not take long to kick in, and gave her just the boost that she needed.

About two and a half hours later, she found herself finishing the last of lecture eight's notes. She was tired from the long day, but was relieved not to be dozing off, despite the weight under her eyes kicking in. As such, she felt it best to take a few extra minutes to skim over all of the notes to gauge her retention. To her surprise, she had remembered just about all of the material that she had focused on. The four and a half hours had really paid off. By the time that her book was back in her bag, her laptop was closed, and her laundry was hung or folded, her smart watch read 12:10 AM. It was a late night, but not unreasonably so, as she did not have to be awake until 8:30 AM or so. Her step count also read 10,763, so all of that running around ended up paying off in the end.

As she got ready for the next day, getting prepped for sleep and putting all of her electronics on their respective chargers, she got into bed and reflected on the past day. She was amazed not only at how productive it had ended up being, but at how she dodged so many potential procrastination potholes that would have been so easy to fall into. Thanks to her efficiency and determination this evening, she spent the remaining few minutes of her waking day fantasizing about what she would do with the next few free nights that she would subsequently have. She conjured a few social opportunity ideas with her friends, as well as getting to finally go back to the gym that she had neglected due to schoolwork.

All-in-all, it was a great day, and she couldn't wait to wake back up and start a fresh new day.

Looking at this scenario, you may be wondering why there are so many particularities and details to the story. After all, it is just a fictitious scenario of a student studying. So what? We've all been there. Fair enough, but these particular, seemingly menial details come together to give us a lot of information about the student's personality, character, academic performance, and especially her values. Let us break the whole thing down and see how they apply. As you read through this, feel free to relate these traits and characteristics to yourself. What do you do similarly? What do you do differently? Could you find more success in taking a page from her book? Would her techniques make things more difficult for you? Consider these questions and others as you internalize what you read.

First, let us consider the most obvious question that remains: was this truly a productive day, or was it a complete train wreck? It seemed as if so much happened that it would wipe anyone out, though the student stuck through it and completed what she sought out to accomplish. In all reality, she completed even more than simply taking the evening to study. Look back on everything that was completed by the time she got to bed: attending two classes, completing a five-hour shift at work, getting over 10,000 steps in, eating meals, watching television, studying for somewhere between four and a half and five hours, completing two loads of laundry, folding and hanging her clean clothes, and topping everything off by getting eight hours of sleep. Despite getting locked out of her room, she still managed to get everything she needed done in style, freeing up the next few evenings. If this is not a productive evening, or a productive day overall, I don't know what is.

Breaking down each accomplishment, was the amount of time that she devoted to studying enough? After all, she had sought out to devote the entire evening to studying, yet she did not end up studying the whole night. However, consider what chore she chose to do between study sessions: laundry. What is the one characteristic of laundry that is set apart from all other household chores? It is periodically addressed. You throw a load of clothes into the washing machine, then wait. When that has completed washing, the clothes are transferred to the dryer, and another gap in time occurs. Our heroine was smart and efficient with her time. She may have forgotten about her laundry and rushed out of the room in this scenario, but it was during the break that she was already on. The most tedious part of doing laundry, folding and hanging, was not done until she had completed her studying for the evening.

On top of all of this, her efficiency and effectiveness in studying was most observable when she reviewed all of her notes at the end of her studying and found that she had retained all (or at least most) of the information that she had focused on. It should be easy for most people to review their study notes and gauge whether or not they properly absorbed the information reviewed, especially if they took proper notes and paid attention during the teacher's lectures. Thus, it is fair to conclude that the student was indeed effective with her study time.

What of her overall productivity? Was there a sense of neglect for anything else that she needed to complete that evening? Were there any glaring issues with her choice of what to do? The scenario does make mention of the student neglecting her time at the gym due to all of her academic commitments. As stated, part of having a value system requires you to disperse your time to the things that are the most important to you. For this student, academic success is more important than getting to work out every day, which is a positive value system. After all, college tuition would be an awfully expensive gym membership if it took precedence over studies. Nonetheless, the student prioritized getting her daily steps in as a means of compensation for the time that she foresaw putting into her studies.

There is little indication of how clean or messy her dorm room was, or its usual status most of the time. However, there is mention that she used a disinfectant wipe to clean off her desk after eating dinner. This implies that the student is very diligent in keeping her space clean, especially when you take into consideration that this was completed immediately after eating, not even a few minutes later. Something as seemingly simple as the added detail of the student disposing of the wipe after using it indicates cleanliness, as many people struggle to even throw trash away after using it. Someone who did not value cleanliness could have just as easily left that wipe lying on the desk that it had just cleaned. Additionally, her choice to complete laundry during study breaks as opposed to fiddling with her phone or completing another leisurely activity also implies that the values of cleanliness and organization are both important to her.

What does this story tell us about the student's social life? Does she value her friendships, and is she able to get along in social environments? Although most of the scenario takes place while she is by herself in her dorm room, there are a number of hints that indicate her ability to socialize. Firstly, she is employed at a nearby grocery store. Although her exact position at the store is not specified, there are very few positions that do not deal with customers to some extent, thus promoting the value of customer service. Even if she had a position that was entirely secluded from customers, working at a grocery store requires interactions with many coworkers in different departments throughout, so little isolated work would occur. Next, when she was locked out of her room, she did not hesitate to try and find her suitemates or her hall's RA. When neither of these worked, she went straight for the dormitory's main lobby and asked for help. Though the specifics of how she felt about having to do this were not specified, it is probably safe to conclude that she has no problem with encountering people when need be, even if the conversation is not fun. Waiting ten minutes for the lazy RA was undoubtedly too long, though the student's mind may have simply wandered into a daydreaming state. Either way, she was able to shake it off and confront the RA to get what she needed, and she did indeed get back into her room without waiting any longer. Finally, the end of the scenario left our heroine falling asleep, fantasizing about meeting up with her friends and doing something fun. Clearly, much of tonight's motivation was fueled by her desire to clear her schedule to have fun, and she seemed most invested in doing so with the people she cared about, not isolated in her dorm room. It should be apparent that this student does not have a problem with encountering people and enjoys socialization. However, just as was the case with going to the gym, she was more than prepared to put her academics first over the fun times that others would sooner reach out for.

Did your perspective on the student change when she forgot her key card in her room and got locked out? Was there a part of you that suddenly thought a little less of her? It is the hope of this author that you did not come out of this story with less of an opinion of her, certainly not at this point in the book. The student may be organized and on top of things, but she is also a human being, prone to making mistakes just like any of us. In fact, it was her drive and motivation that resulted in her forgetting the key entirely. Her quick thinking in running off to transfer her laundry came as a result of her thoughtfulness and focus on what needed to be done. Everyone makes mistakes. Plus, nothing ever goes EXACTLY as it was planned. There are always some changes or interferences, whether in or out of the planner's control. To be fair, the student also addressed this matter immediately after it occurred, and it was resolved in a matter of minutes. Had the head RA done her job correctly, or had either of her suitemates or hall's RA been present, it would have been resolved in seconds. Life is unpredictable, and things like this are unavoidable. As a result, one's success ought not to be measured by the mistakes. Rather, success ought to be assessed based on what was done as a result to fix them. It's not about how one falls, but more so about how they get back up.

Author's Experience

The scenario in this chapter deliberately notes the student's organizational abilities with the notes that she had taken on her laptop. This is a practice that I started to employ when I was in college. Having one big folder that contained the contents of my entire college experience proved to be extremely useful, as it helped keep everything in one place, not scattered all over my computer's desktop. As also described in the scenario, subfolders represented each year, then within the years were each semester. Finally, within the semester folders was one folder for each class I had enrolled in. I'm sure it sounds tedious and extensive, but it makes a lot of sense once created. Plus, each semester's folder allowed for any other documents that needed to be saved, such as financial aid paperwork or digital copies of other important documents.

Unfortunately, two years' worth of content was lost when my laptop irreparably crashed, causing me to lose absolutely all of my work. Thankfully, the stores were running some tech sales for students, so my sister and I were able to get brand-new MacBooks, as her similar model of laptop had coincidentally crashed at the same time. I know what you're thinking, and no: we did not collaborate to break our computers to get new ones!

This process of organizing papers, notes, syllabi, and any other relevant documents carried over onto my new laptop, and it proved to be a foolproof way to keep everything in one place, while taking no time at all to either create or manage. However, there was one problem: I was a terrible note-taker. If my mind didn't wander off into songwriting land, I had a tendency to resort to writing short stories or getting onto social media. This was obviously a very bad habit, and it got the best of me when test time came around, as I had to try and figure out what content would be covered. Some classes did not even include a textbook, and were solely based on the information covered in each lecture, so I struggled with tests and spontaneous quizzes for many years. The importance of keeping everything organized on your phone, tablet, and/or laptop is so important, and sometimes cannot be learned until a detrimental mistake is made.

Although I can proudly claim that I am very well organized today, especially on all of my devices, I am still not impervious to the pain of losing vital information. All of my devices share files on a cloud, which are instantly accessible wherever I go that has Internet. Everything is interchangeable between my phone, tablet, and laptop. If there is no available Wi-Fi, I can pull my phone out and work on it. If the device that I was using needs to charge, I can place it down to charge, then resume right where I left off on another one. Better yet, everything is saved automatically without me having to worry about incessantly hitting a "save" button. Perfect, right? Not so much.

In writing this very book, I took several hours on a Sunday to sit down and write, putting everything aside just as our heroine in the scenario did. My tablet's screen was shared between the contents of my book thus far and my detailed outline. At times, it almost seemed as if I would finish the book that evening at the rate I was going, typing thousands of words.

Finally, I decided that it was time for a break, as my tablet's battery was slowly dying anyway. Checking the top button that read "Autosave," I made sure that it was time-stamped with the most recent few minutes to include my latest changes, and it appeared to have done so. As such, I took it over to the charger, plugged it in, and sat back down with my phone. Within two or three minutes, I was getting anxious to return to typing, so I opened the document. To my horror, some 3,000 words had gone missing! Part of me wasn't too worried about it, thinking that the tablet just needed a second to sync with the cloud. Checking it out, I went back to the tablet and opened the document. My stomach dropped as I saw that the lower word-count had synchronized onto the tablet as well. All of that work, all of those ideas, all of those hours of my precious weekend…gone, just like that.

Part of me wanted to throw something across the room! In all seriousness, I kept my composure, but was nevertheless heartbroken. How could this have happened?! I knew that I had checked that it had saved! After taking another hour to search around each device, as well as my cloud files, I finally accepted the fact that my work had evaporated into cyberspace, never to be found again. Incidentally, I was with my significant other when all of this happened, and she (of course) knew just what I needed to hear. Without skipping a beat, she related this incident to a recent incident where she lost four of the seven pages of a paper she had worked on tirelessly for days. However, she managed to quickly type up what she recalled as missing just before class, and still managed to receive a positive grade on the paper.

With this encouragement, I put the book aside for a day to try and relax, as I also came to accept that my fuel tank had hit empty for the day. After work the following day, I sat down and outlined everything that I had written in excruciating detail, and found that it all came back to me very naturally and quickly. Sure enough, just as my significant other had predicted would happen, I managed to write everything that had initially taken me several hours in less than one!

While technology is an amazing tool to those who know how to use it, the devastation of losing the progress we have clawed for can sometimes feel like the end of the world. For that reason, learn from my error and go the extra mile to make sure that you have properly saved your work. Despite the amazing autosave feature that most word processing applications have, send yourself a copy of your progress, or back it up on another file. Technology is great and convenient in most cases, but it will never be flawless. Get into the habit of saving your work. Don't allow for any margin of error, human or otherwise.

In conclusion, much was said about this student and her values overall. The way someone distributes their time is the ultimate way of expressing values. Again, think about what is important to you. Do video games take precedence over the books? Do social opportunities on Saturday or Sunday take priority over expressing your religious values? Is watching the halftime report of the game you already watched more important than talking with your significant other or other loved ones? I as the author cannot tell you what you do, or should, value most or least in your life; nor do I have the ability or authority to tell you how to spend your time. Rather, you are encouraged to give time to that which you care about. After all, there is no better way to show how much you care than to shut everything else off.

Chapter 8:
The Tangibles of Time Management

If you have taken the time to determine what your value system consists of, and you understand the importance of expressing those values by dispersing your time accordingly, then it is time to help you do so in an organized and cohesive manner.

What came to your mind when you read the title of this book? Did it conjure images of planners, sticky notes, binders, Manila envelopes, folders, and other tools used for academic organization? What did you expect to find within the book? Tips on how to sort this or alphabetize that? If this was the case for you, then this section is for you.

This chapter of the book will discuss some of the ways in which you can make the most of organization, as related to time management. As the title suggests, we will try and focus on tangible tasks and means that can be completed, focusing less on the mindset as other chapters did. As this chapter begins, start to think about what you have or have not done leading up to this point in your academic career. Reflect on things that you might have tried, but did not turn out to be as successful as you had hoped. Perhaps there was an idea that you employed, or that a parent or teacher recommended for you, and you were pleasantly surprised at how well it worked for you. Keep in mind that electronics (apps, reminders, etc.) are going to be operationally considered as "tangible" for this chapter, so do not hesitate to take these into consideration as well.

In approaching this subject, it is important to reiterate the recurring disclaimer that this book does not seek to correct what works for you. If you have developed a system that works well for you and contradicts the messages of this book, then more power to you! It is not the objective of anything in here to correct you if you are successful. In fact, the book does not even particularly seek to show you HOW to do something. No two people do something the exact same way, and that is one of the beauties and majestic parts of the diversity of the human mind. The points in this book are only here to serve as a jumping-off point to help you start on the exploration of what techniques work best for you. With all of that in mind, let's get right to it.

Whereas other parts of this book require intricate discussions and lengthy scenarios to communicate major points, there are a few key points that can be identified when searching for the most effective tools of time management and task completion. The one overall point that should be the goal of everyone trying to develop in this area is that an effective tool will help you get your tasks done, plain and simple. There is no need to make things complicated.

Think about it: if you try to do something and it doesn't work, why keep trying it? Get rid of it, and try something different! As has been repeated so many times, different things work for different people. No single technique is going to be universally effective, so why waste your time with "foolproof methods?" Get rid of anything and everything that does not work. The chapter could end here, but we'll give you a little more to work with.

Next, consider: what is easily accessible for you? Are there things you already have and would not require additional money for you or a loved one to spend? If you do not have access to something, consider some cheap things to try, such as sticky notes. Many people claim that you should have a notebook for each class instead of one big one for everything. Others go so far as to say that you should have a different backpack for each day of the week. This is admittedly a bit over the top, especially considering the section earlier that discussed making the most of your storage organization. However, no disrespect is intended if this technique works, or ends up working, best for you.

Take a second to get your phone and/or tablet out. Look at all of the different applications. Think about how many of these you actually use. Are there any opportunities to delete a few and make some room in your phone? Getting rid of visual clutter might free up the opportunity to convert your device into the tool that it was initially created for. Some of the basic features that every smartphone comes with include a calendar, reminders, alarms, alerts and custom notifications, task lists and check lists, an application for notes, and more. Most phones have some form of an artificial intelligence system that serves as a simulated assistant. A common feature of these is the ability for a user to ask the digital assistant to create calendar appointments, reminders, alarms, tasks, etc., all with just a few key words. Take the time to go on the Internet and learn how to speak to your device in particular, as each one works off of specific terms and phrases. Most programs should even be able to operate working off of ear buds or headphones, making it even more accessible to use. All of this is just part of the learning process, as you may find that your devices are not helpful to you whatsoever.

Is there anything in your room or workspace, maybe hanging on a wall or door, that allows you to write or pin things up? After all, electronic tools can be so easily ignored and neglected when they go off. However, there seems to be something so much more difficult about crumpling a piece of paper with a task on it, or maybe erasing an item on a white board before it has been completed. Doing so is more intense, as it cannot be recovered or undone like an electronic item. Erasing something or scribbling it out is permanent, so you may find yourself more obligated to keep it up.

With all of these points in mind, let us list and discuss three main components of an effective time management tool:

1. Any tool that allows you to continue to modify when needed.
2. Any tool that catches your eye and is difficult to ignore or neglect, whether deliberately or accidentally.
3. Any tool that brings you a sense of satisfaction when tasks are completed.

These may seem strange to you, but there is something to be said about the power that something seemingly inanimate can have over you. It is almost as if there needs to be a mutual respect between you and whatever time management tool you find to be most effective for you. You should be intimidated by the item and its presence. If you opt to use sticky notes, the presence of those yellow slips of paper all over your desk should be unsettling, making you want to address and complete the tasks that are contained on them. Should you resort to using a task list on your phone, the presence of all of those checklist items ought to have an anxious effect on you. The sight of them should be uncomfortable enough to motivate their completion.

With all of these proposed effects that the tangible has on the mental state, you should develop a sense of confidence in yourself. These tools are not here to make you do the work any better. They are merely there to tell you what to do and, possibly, when it needs to be done. Just a reminder. At the end of the day, you are the one who has gotten this far in your academic career, not that sticky note or white board marker. You have to believe in yourself and your ability to get through the tough times. You can, and you will. Everyone has their fears, and everyone doubts their own abilities from time to time. However, these tools are there to remind you what to do, only because you CAN do it. If you were not able to, there would be nothing to remind you of.

Author's Experience

As mentioned in the Author's Experience of the last chapter, I used to struggle with taking strong, quality notes. Despite having the technology, the organizational skills, and the time in class to do so, I struggled with both focusing and taking concise, solid notes. Regardless of the format that I used to take notes, whether pen and paper or on my laptop, my notes were almost entirely incomprehensible. Either I would write these little words and phrases without any context, or I would focus on adding too much detail to one point and I would miss the next five points. Just the other day, I happened across an old spiral-bound notebook from my final year in college and took a few minutes to flip through it. I was shocked at just how incomprehensible most of it was: just absolute gobbledygook. The only pages that made some sense were the random guitar tabs or sets of song lyrics that I had written instead of paying attention in class.

Much of this chapter has taken the time to reiterate the value of tangible time management tools. This is another area that I struggled in for a long time, and nothing seemed to work for me. Calendar notifications on my phone, sticky notes, a large desk drawer calendar, even a tack board that took up my whole dorm room wall—nothing I tried to implement seemed to work for me, and I could not seem to figure out why, for the life of me. It wasn't until I had exhausted seemingly every option that I came across an obvious one that I had yet to try: a dry erase board.

Something about the idea initially seemed outlandish to me, as it seemed more appropriate for a teacher's classroom than a student's dorm room. Then it occurred to me why nothing had worked so far. Truthfully, nothing seemed easy and quick to update and customize. Sure, the other items were nice to have sitting around the room or on my phone, but it took some effort. With a sticky note, you could only fit so much on one note before having to add to another one, especially since I always liked adding extra details to my tasks. With a paper calendar, there was the similar issue of limited writing space. On top of that, you could never change anything without scribbling something out, and that just looked sloppy.

On an electronic calendar, it was tedious to have to add each individual task that needed to be completed in one day, or even just one evening. Plus, the worst part was that as phones and electronics advanced, it became progressively easier to either get distracted from a task by getting sucked into an application, or just swipe and ignore any incoming notifications. These barriers were all immediately trumped by the white board.

With even just a small white board crudely mounted over my corner desk, I was able to keep track of not only the tasks needed for each day, but even having the chance to take quick notes of whatever I was working on. If I had a paper to write, I would manually scribble the drafted outline onto the board and have it within sight as I typed on my laptop. If need be, I could add a side note in a different color to make it pop out. Perhaps the best part of it was the satisfaction that came from crossing an item off once it had been completed. Even just finishing a few sentences of a paper warranted crossing off a section of its coinciding outline. Sometimes, just for the pure joy of having completed a task, I would slowly cross the item off, letting the marker tip screech its way across the board. This goes back to the benefits of having a tangible time management item, as it helps you perceive the completion of your task through sensory elements. The feel of the small, cool marker, the sounds and squeaks of it dancing across the task, the sight of its color trail documenting my success, and the smell of the ink all came together to help me feel a sense of accomplishment.

Within the last two weeks or so of each semester, the white board became an incredible asset to finishing the term strong. As the end came within reach, I would erase everything on the board and replace it with every academic task that stood between me and summer or winter break. There were times that I would start early, and it would appear more like a black board from all of the writing that I had to do. Doing this proved to be one of the most effective factors in helping me reach the end successfully, as I had everything I needed right in front of me. As my friends would come and go from my dorm room or apartment (depending on the year), seeing these remaining tasks would inspire and remind them that the end was in sight. One friend even followed my beat and wrote down everything left for his own semester, and he found it extremely motivating.

To this day, I find this process to be the most effective in accomplishing multiple tasks. Even still, I have a sizable dry erase white board on the inside of my closet, giving me quick access to jot down miscellaneous things that need to be done. In terms of keeping track of work and writing projects, I have switched to using a tablet and smart pencil. This allows me to take the list to different locations where it might be needed, as I often write while on the go. Nevertheless, it is my hope that you find your equivalency to the white board. Who knows? Maybe a white board is just what you need.

Organizing homework has changed as computers, tablets, and phones have continued to play a progressively bigger role in academia. Not long ago was the time where computers and laptops were mainly just used for word processing and research on the Internet. Before, everything had to be done manually: typewriter or pen and paper, and actual research in a physical library with a mountain of books and periodicals. In the era of your collegiate career, you are privileged to also be able to submit your work online, as well as take part in interactive online classes, all on platforms that are easy to learn and use for most people. Take full advantage of this. In the same way that you can make sure your workspace is flooded with reminders of all that needs to be done, see about any features that are hard to avoid on your laptop. Most laptops should have some sort of free application or pre-programmed feature that allows you to put customized notes on your desktop. If you have the discipline to keep updating these notes, they will be staring right at you as you begin to give in to the temptation to watch something on a streaming site or play a video game. The portability of all of the electronic devices that many college students own means that the potential for efficiency and the utilization of time management tools is just as portable and accessible.

By this point in your life, it is probably safe to say that you have found some form of alarm that effectively wakes you up in the morning. Is it a song from your phone, or maybe a classic manual alarm clock with bells? Perhaps you use a white noise machine to fall asleep and wake up to soothing sounds from some faraway paradise. No matter the source, it has proven to work for you at one point or another. Some people struggle to fight the alarm's call, hitting the "snooze" button repeatedly and growing later by increments of nine minutes at a time. In this way, try to set reminders for yourself when a particularly important task is due. Try to make it so that ignoring these reminders is virtually impossible. Play around with the settings to see how strong you can make each alert. These do not necessarily have to be loud, obnoxious notifications. Rather, something as subtle as a vibration in your pocket may be enough to get your attention, thinking it is a friend or loved one trying to contact you. Tricking yourself might result in some frustration, though it is hard for many of us to ignore a phone notification, so go ahead and lie to yourself.

Speaking of waking up in the morning, it is probably also safe to assume that you have discovered whether or not you function better in the mornings or evenings. Is it easy for you to get up early and complete homework or go to the gym, or does such a thought make you anxious since it would interfere with the option to stay up late? Many people already know this about themselves, and have adjusted their daily schedules accordingly. On a separate note, taking this into consideration is important when registering for classes; not only for factors such as your attendance and punctuality, but also for how well your brain works overall. If you are irreparably foggy in the morning where even coffee itself does nothing to help immediately, maybe classes at 8:00 in the morning are not such a good idea. Similarly, if you have found that you thrive more in the morning, consider scheduling all or most of your classes in the morning. Get them out of the way to allow for more time in the afternoon for other things.

A common justification for procrastinating is "I'll just get up early tomorrow and do it." Funnily enough, this is a legitimate process for some people. In fact, many insist that their brains function better when they first wake up. For others, the late nights are just the fix to help them get what they need done effectively. In any event, finishing an assignment in the morning should have more justification than that you've gotten bored. It should be prefaced by a yawn and a stretch, indicating that the body cannot take much more information. Should you need to return to your commitments in the morning, try leaving everything you had out in order to help you return to the exact state of mind you were in when you started studying that evening.

This technique just goes back to knowing yourself, and determining which method works best for you. However, you cannot truly determine what works best for you until you try out different things, so try to spend your first semester in college testing out different times and methods to see which suits you. With that said, do not wait until a big deadline or the night before a test to try it out. Rather, take an evening of low pressure and try waking up early. Once you find what works best for you, try your best to stay consistent with it to ensure some level of discipline and proper expectations for yourself.

An idea that has arisen many times in this book is that true and proper time management can only be obtained once other components in life are in order, and I stand by this. How can one expect, or be expected, to keep an organized and functional schedule if the items within their schedule are not being managed on their own? Furthermore, what good is time management at all if someone proves to be unable to keep things together?

When considering these ideas, the phrase "clean and organized" comes to mind. It is so common to speak of something being "clean and organized" and, although lumped together, they are truly two completely different variables. For instance, one can show tremendous success at keeping their dorm room clean. Their floor always remains spotless and crumb-free, and all surfaces are clear of clutter. At the same time, they have no idea where anything is. There are no designated spaces for anything, and they are losing or misplacing something almost daily. Such a case would be an example of cleanliness without organization. On the other hand, you might have someone who neglects any and all responsibility when it comes to keeping things clean. Piles of dirty clothes flood their room, and old dishes pile up on the counter near the room's sink. Bug traps in the corner of the room still contain dormitory roaches from three weeks ago, and the trash can is overflowing into the main floorspace. However, when it comes to their homework, everything is sorted into labeled folders and binders, never losing a single item. This would clearly be a case of organization without cleanliness.

Such as in this example, the key to mastering the concept of "time management" is to be able to properly separate the words "time" and "management," addressing them each on their own. They may come together, but only once they have been properly addressed in their own respective manners.

A similar example can be found in the phrase "working hard." This is a difficult one to hear or say for any manager, as an employee who is underperforming might defend themselves under the guise of "working hard" or "always going out of (their) way" for the company. A stereotypical response from a manager might be, "I see you are working hard, but not working smart." This is not a pleasant phrase to hear from your supervisor, no matter the intention on their end. No one, at least with any kind of work ethic, enjoys hearing that the way they put forth their best efforts is insufficient.

Nevertheless, the unfortunate truth is that there are not many cases in which a boss or supervisor is saying something like this simply to bully their employees. The pain and frustration that is felt when hearing something of this nature should be a wake-up call. After all, what it all comes down to is that hard work should not come first. It may sound weird, even crazy, to hear someone put down the value of hard work. Do not be mistaken, hard work is an extremely important factor and characteristic which, tragically, is quickly becoming more and more of a hot commodity. However, the better characteristic to master is that of efficiency. One can both work hard and work efficiently.

Think of it this way: imagine you have a huge Excel spreadsheet, full to the brim with thousands of names, addresses, phone numbers, emails, and other information. Adding to and formatting a spreadsheet like that takes so much time, effort and concentration, even if you know all of the tricks to Excel. Now imagine that under the names, everything is formatted "Last Name, First Name" and your boss asks for it to be changed so that there are separate cells for the first and last names, respectively.

Let us now approach this from a purely "hard working" perspective. An employee might hear this and dedicate their afternoon to manually typing out each individual name into their own cells. As a result of taking the time to do this, they had to neglect an important email that came in from a higher-up in the company, forgot about a meeting that they were asked to take minutes for, and missed a call that they had been waiting for from a potential client. Unfortunately, they did not even get a chance to finish this undertaking by the end of the workday, and stayed until 10:00 in the evening to get this done.

Now let's look at another scenario. This same task was given to a second employee, who wanted to save the time and effort that typing manually would take. Instead of wasting time, they took the time to search online for any tools built into the software to be able to complete the task instantly. The employee found a video walking through the steps; and though it took about six minutes to watch the video and walk through the steps on the spreadsheet, a few clicks later resulted in all of the names being transferred into their respective columns. As a result of getting this task done so quickly, they were able to move onto their emails, meetings, and even managed to get ahead on a few calls that they had to make the following day. By the time they left the office, they were in shock about how efficient the day had turned out.

Which of these two scenarios turned out to be the more effective one? The "hard worker," or the more efficient worker? It is probably apparent that the second worker came out on top, but why? Clearly, they managed to get more done in one workday, but does this make them a hard worker, or is the first worker who was dedicated and focused the harder worker?

This is actually a difficult question to answer, as it is somewhat subjective. To someone who is not familiar with computers in general, much less Excel, it seems like the first worker really went out of their way to get this done. If their supervisor in particular is not too familiar with Excel, it would certainly seem that the first worker's methods were the only way and worthy of commending. Additionally, some work environments are slow-moving, resulting in many workers looking for something to do. In such a case, it would appear pretty dedicated to spend this much time and focus on that undertaking. However, the second worker shows a substantial and important attribute that was not highlighted: a willingness to learn. This employee internally acknowledged that they did not know a certain skill, and was ready to develop by learning how to perform a function not only for this task, but for any relevant future projects as well.

This is what time management is really all about. The beauty of it goes beyond the customizability of a schedule, or the ability to use whatever techniques and characteristics work best for you. At the end of the day, everything comes down to being able and willing to learn and develop. Anybody that claims to have everything down is either lying to you or themselves. As was stated earlier in this book, trying different things and seeing what works best for you is essential, but also being willing to acknowledge areas that need improvement and learning from them is the only characteristic that will inevitably ensure advancement.

Are both of these employees hard workers? From the information we were given, it certainly seems that way. Though they went home at different times, both had accomplished the mutual task at hand by the time they walked through their own front doors. Some might argue that each simply have their own separate methods of approaching tasks, their own styles and approaches. Fair enough. However, consider the following analogy and apply it to this situation.

Within the field of mental health, an absolutely vital ability that every clinician must bear is that of determining whether or not someone has a disability. Although not all clinicians are legally authorized to diagnose someone, they very much should be able to tell the differences between someone who has a mental health disability and someone who is eccentric or possibly going through a difficult time. One of the main determining factors is that of general functionality. How much of whatever behavior is considered "odd" or "abnormal" is interfering with the functioning of the individual in question? In other words, is a certain behavior getting in the way of the person being able to carry out their daily tasks?

For example, let's say a student walks into a therapist's office for the first time, simply saying that they are feeling "depressed," and that they think they might have depression. Doing a 25-minute evaluation, one question that the therapist asks about is that of their daily routines, and whether or not the student is able to carry out basic functions and complete everything that they are responsible for (homework, work shift, etc.). The student answers that they are indeed able to keep themselves clean and their dorm room orderly, and they have not missed any school or work as a result of their "down-in-the-dumps" feelings. After some more questions, the therapist finds that the student does not have major depressive disorder or any other variant of clinical depression.

Yes, I know that this example feels like it was out of left field. However, let's apply it to the example of the two workers and see what happens.

As we are not evaluating the mental health stability and functionality of these two employees, we must first change the phrasing of the question. Instead of questioning their ability to function normally within society, we could instead phrase it to ask this: "Is the method being utilized enough to interfere with the other tasks at work?" Is this technique working effectively, or is it starting to slow me down? Am I still able to complete all of my other tasks for the day, or is this project consuming the time that I would normally use for those tasks?

Looking at the scenario with the first worker, it is safe to say that it did indeed consume the rest of their day, which is especially problematic since the second worker proved that to be completely unnecessary. The second worker completed the task in a little less than ten minutes, versus the worker who took literal hours to get this done. Yes, there is no doubt that these two people both work hard at their similar jobs. However, as has been continuously demonstrated (but has yet to be firmly stated), hard work and efficiency are not necessarily correlated.

These examples have been stepping outside of the realm of college life. Consider, though, that college is merely preparation for all that is encountered in the real world. When preparing for college, you should be mentally preparing for so much more than just another level of your education. As has been preached continuously throughout our journey together, the practices that you establish during your collegiate career are inevitably going to carry over into the work world. This is not to suggest that there is not always an opportunity for growth and development, but the old proverb still rings true: old habits die hard.

Author's Experience

So many of these Author's Experience segments have discussed my weak points in the past, and this is no accident. I personally take more out of stories where somebody made a mistake or just messed everything up in a particular scenario. As such, I want to save you as the reader from the same mistakes that I have made over the years.

In a previous Author's Experience segment, I mentioned that I worked as a case manager right out of college, and even mentioned that the company's managerial techniques were not the best. This is an understatement, as they were so aggressive toward their workers; yet different managers always seemed to provide different statements and inconsistent information. Before my favorite and long-time program manager was transferred to another county branch, she was loved by her employees because she was all about positive reinforcement. She was a huge advocate for her workers, providing suggestions for development in a positive and supportive way. This was the same for the county's on-staff clinician, with whom the program manager worked very closely and, as a result, was almost like a second manager within her role. Overall, it was a really happy and energetic place to work. Similar to my program manager, one of the two head directors of the company was a very kind-hearted and soft-spoken man, who worked alongside a very energetic and focused woman. The two were known to work extremely well together, and most could witness how they would balance each other out, even during staff meetings.

Coincidentally, around the time that the male director stepped down from his position, my program manager was transferred to another county to assist with her extensive commute. The male director was not replaced, and the female director very quickly proved herself to be a very aggressive leader when by herself. Her friendly demeanor in staff meetings faded, program managers were put under tremendous pressure to be harder on case managers, and case managers were also put under extraordinary pressure due to the high turnover rate from people quitting (the average turnover rate was about three to five months). As a result of the company refusing to have a waitlist, each case manager had 40-50 clients on their caseload, being expected to see all of them or document extremely detailed encounters for each of them on a weekly basis. This was unheard of, as each case manager's usual quota was about 20 visits per week.

While with the company I wore many different hats over the years: case manager for adults, care coordinator for children, intakes for adults, intakes for children, reassessments for adults, reassessments for children, and training new hires as needed. Each one of these responsibilities required extensive training and practice and demanded a different method of documentation. At the point when there were the least number of workers in our county's office, a manager who was known to have an aggressive attitude was brought in to assist with "setting our county straight." One day, she sat down with the program manager of the county at that time and each worker, and she gave her two cents' worth on how each one was "working hard, not working smart."

Although I have always been very understanding when presented with room for improvement, I refused to accept this meeting, and I spoke up in a way that I had not done in the past. I admittedly felt my blood start to boil, and my Cuban genetic temper was starting to set in, as she went on and on about how my methods were not sufficient, even despite my number of visits being consistently high and my documentation being extensively detailed. As she started to take more cheap shots, the Cuban tension came to a climax, and I interrupted her, "Okay, hold on a minute." I proceeded to do what I could to defend myself and my coworkers, though she did not remain silent. Although it was not a yelling match, there was definitely a lot of tension in the conversation, rendering my program manager completely speechless.

Later that day after the second manager had left, I went into my program manager's office and apologized for being unprofessional. I was shocked when she proceeded to demand that I retract my apology, as she felt as if nothing of what I said in there, no matter how strongly it was presented, was at all inappropriate. Nothing I said was directed at anyone, no obscenities were used, and I was not out of line in defending myself.

In hindsight, I look at this experience and am glad that I defended myself, as this second manager and I developed a positive working relationship, and there was a mutual respect that came over time. She was even part of hiring me for a promotion a few months later, and she came to me for a few developmental projects that she needed feedback on after others had dropped the ball. Although she and I never directly addressed that meeting, she and I spoke often about our

respective cultures—mine Cuban, and hers Puerto Rican—
and how there were so many similarities between the two. My
own conviction is that because of our similar backgrounds, she
was understanding of the fire that came out of me that day, as
it had come out of her as well. Additionally, as mentioned,
everyone in that room had a different perspective of how
management was changing entirely, despite it not being
addressed explicitly.

With all of that said, I am not presenting this story to
you to encourage you to be aggressive toward your superiors.
Rather, I am warning you that I was extremely lucky in this
situation, and was likely let off of the hook because of my
history of being nothing but open-minded and respectful
toward my superiors. Had this been more of an ongoing issue,
it likely would have backfired. Nevertheless, if you feel as if
you are being targeted by a teacher, supervisor, manager, or
other authority figure, make sure to present your concerns in
a professional manner. If you can, address them as they arise,
not in hindsight, and prioritize evidence over emotion. No one
enjoys being in these types of situations, but they do occur,
even in school. It is best that you be prepared and work your
hardest so that you are indeed able to defend yourself.

One of the best values that needs to be mentioned on
the subject of academic and professional development is how
to approach a situation that you do not have an answer for.
Perhaps this is a scenario where you just recently started
working for a retailer, and a customer asks to return a sweater
that has a black ink stain on it. You know that the store has a
30-day return policy, but the black stain is suspicious, and you
wonder if this item is shoplifted, as the customer claims to
have lost their receipt as well. What should you do?

First, there is nothing wrong with saying, "I don't know" when faced with a difficult situation. You may have started a job years ago and have developed so much experience, and still encounter things that you have never seen before. Just as job environments change, just as academic settings and content changes, just as "general knowledge" develops, so will the inquiries and challenges that you will be faced with. It is rare for someone's knowledge base to become stagnant as a result of the work environment not changing at all. As such, be willing to ask questions and develop in the environment and your field as a whole.

You may be wondering how the academic field is changing, as it seems as if it is fairly consistent with itself for the most part. Just think of the advancements that have taken place to completely change the ways in which we receive an education. Although the Internet is not new, it has become substantially faster and more advanced from the excruciatingly slow dial-up days. Video streams faster and clearer; browser searches are done in a micro-fraction of a second, reaping potentially billions of results; and entire libraries' worth of books, periodicals, and various other pieces of information are all uploaded and instantly downloadable. Look at how the prices of computers has changed. It used to be a substantial investment to purchase a computer, and desktops were the standard. Now laptops are the standard purchase, and affordable ones are reliable and extremely accessible. On top of that, smartphones have become so common that most people have an Android or iPhone, which is more powerful and multifunctional than any computer before a certain date. Even iPads and other tablets have developed to be so powerful that they can feasibly replace a laptop when a keyboard is attached.

Along with the rapid and intense development of powerful and accessible technology, the world around us has also changed. We can now walk into a store without a purse or wallet, simply relying on our phone or smart watch to pay for our groceries or gas. If a new bottle of laundry detergent is needed, all that is necessary is to pick up the phone and go into the Amazon app to repurchase whatever is needed with just a few clicks, and it will be at our doorstep in two days. There are even designated buttons to put around your house that are pressed to instantly reorder an item that is frequently used when it runs out.

With these changes, the ability to complete classes over the Internet has become more than doable. So long as you have a strong enough connection to Wi-Fi or your phone's network, you can easily stream lectures and retrieve your study materials online effortlessly. As discussed, communication is instant, so there is no trouble when needing to reach a teacher or classmate. Group projects can be done over a video call, not even needing to meet in person if you live on campus. For in-person classes, many schools even offer an online portal or dashboard in order to display and submit your documents. The practice of printing a paper out and placing it on your teacher's desk in the morning is about as dated as placing an apple on it.

Furthermore, there are now even satellite campuses that have been developed for regions that are located far from local colleges where it would cause a major inconvenience to anyone trying to make the drive. This is more common for graduate schools, as many graduate students are already in the working world. Many graduate students have been in their own fields for many years and may be older in age, as they are returning to school and not going straight through from college. However, there are plenty of undergraduate programs with the same or similar format.

Regardless, technology has unquestionably changed the normal way in which we live our lives, and these changes are not slowing down anytime soon. It is even going to change the way we engage in transportation every day, as electric vehicles are quickly becoming more accessible and reasonably priced for the general public. There is no way for us to know with certainty the other areas of our lives that will change in the near future, but the change itself is inevitable, and it is best that you are ready to expect that change as it evolves your education.

In discussing time management and balancing all of the different facets of life, one thing that absolutely cannot be left out is that of hobbies and pastimes. This goes beyond the aforementioned television- or movie-watching on Netflix while you are eating dinner in your dorm room. Rather, do you have some sort of a creative outlet that keeps your mind active? Is there something you enjoy doing in your spare time that requires research and intellectual development? Does the activity require the development of fine motor skills? Does it demand that you express yourself in an artistic, unique, and genuine manner? I'm sure that many of us grew up being encouraged to put our energy into something like this: music, reading, painting, drawing, writing, and other creative endeavors.

Have any of these carried over into your adult life? Do you continue to pursue any such activities that force you to develop, or is most of your time dedicated to video games or television? Even something as seemingly simple as working out requires one to read up on different techniques, learn about the way in which the body heals after a workout, develop different nutritional habits to enhance results, and other such topics. Physical fitness is not as simple as lifting up a piece of metal and putting it down. Rather, the extent of success cannot be realized unless there is a true level of focus and learning involved.

What about music? Did you take any lessons for vocals or any musical instruments growing up? Doing so is an incredible outlet as it provides a method of expression, creativity, and even socialization. If you find other people who enjoy what they do as much as you do, if not more, it opens so many opportunities for great friendships and amazing collaborations. When you find a musician that you have creative chemistry with and play with them, there is an amazing bond that is formed through the musical interactions with one another. While improvising, you can often tell where the person is going before they go that way, and vice versa. Finding and developing such a relationship is actually hugely advantageous to your academic career, even if you are not studying music formally. Having one or more musical partners holds you accountable for continuing to develop and expand your mind. Additionally, there is something to be said on behalf of finishing your homework and scheduling out the needed time to work on your musical craft.

The visual artist has a unique advantage over many other hobbies in that a well-developed artist can recreate the images that they conjure in their mind, even if it is simply the environment around them. Visual artists might include painters, sketchers, sculptors, and even graphic designers and bakers. Having a tangible form of expression that can trigger most (if not all) of the senses is incredibly rewarding. However, just as any pastime demands, so much practice and research have to take place to reach a point where full talent can be realized. Nothing comes overnight, and an artist may become discouraged if the outcome of their expressions are less than desirable. Nevertheless, pressing on and learning from mistakes will ensure success if the artist is called toward that medium. In many ways, your imperfections and quirks are what define your particular style.

The hobbies mentioned are certainly not the only ones out there. In reality, the variety of pastimes out there is about as unlimited as you imagine. If you have not found one for yourself, it is never too late to search for one that interests you. In searching for a good one, think of it like a cardio workout. You can walk on the treadmill for hours every day; but if you are walking too slowly to get your heart rate up, it is a complete waste of time. In that same way, make sure to find something that stimulates your intellect, as mentioned before. Try to find something that would require you to read up on it, or to find a community on YouTube of people that create content geared toward that hobby. Spend an hour or two at your local hobby store and see if anything stands out to you. Speak with your friends and see if they have any recommendations for you. After all, most friendships are centered around like-mindedness, and your friends should be able to give you at least some good ideas.

Also, just as earlier advice suggested that you try different things when it came to time management techniques and daily scheduling, you very much ought to try different hobbies and see what fits. Whether it be sports, music, visual art, dancing, or something else, most things require that you get your feet wet in order to truly determine whether or not something will prove to be enjoyable. Additionally, be honest with yourself. If you do not enjoy something, do not try to force yourself to like something that you do not. Instead of wasting time trying to convince yourself that you enjoy something that does not click with you, or trying too hard to enjoy something that you thought you would enjoy for a long time, take that energy and focus on finding an activity more appealing and exciting.

Author's Experience

The last job that I had in college was working for my school's enrollment department. This was a position that I was fortunate enough to have for two and a half years, as I would not have to find other means of income on campus until graduation. Additionally, it was an amazing position that gave me the opportunity to learn about office culture and professionalism early on. I held a few responsibilities within this department, the first being a student recruiter. In training to do so, our managers told us that the most important thing we could keep in mind while reaching out to people (as much of our responsibilities were over-the-phone and documenting interactions) was that there is nothing wrong with saying, "I don't know."

They further explained that everyone will always be prone to encountering questions that are either new to them or they just simply do not know the answer to, if not both. They even encouraged us to assure the person on the other line that though we were not sure of the exact answer to the inquiry, we would follow up with them after speaking with a manager, as this would validate the person's feelings and give them a sense of appreciation. Sure enough, whenever on the phone lines, letting the potential students and their families know that I would follow up on their deeper-cut questions was never met with any hostility or annoyance, much to my initial surprise.

This was a lesson that carried with me into all of my future jobs, and it remained true, even in the toughest of situations. When I worked as an intake specialist for the case management company that I mentioned in an earlier Author's Experience segment, there would be times where I would be completing a reassessment with someone who was angry and frustrated. As our target population was within a generally more severe crowd, there was much more tension when someone was temperamental, and it was absolutely essential to be able to pull all of the tools out of our belt to try and encourage them to stay calm. Even in the toughest of meetings, I would never pretend to know something if I was not certain of the answer. In these instances, I would fluff up my typical answer and boost their egos a bit. Here's what it would look like most of the time:

"That's actually a great question; and believe it or not, you're the first to ask it. Tell you what, I'll speak with (always using my manager's first name, to make their interactions with the company feel more natural and familial, and less formal) and get back to you on that one. I'm pulling up my calendar appointment with you, and just making note of that. Okay, great, does this sound about right to you (read the written question back to them)? Sounds good. I'll shoot you a text at the number that we were texting on. Does that work for you?"

This is quite a bit of dialogue, but keep in mind that the way in which I would say it was just as important, if not more so, in helping keep them calm and feel respected. The way it was transcribed also sounds cheesy and forced, but again, the way it was said was the key to making it feel natural. There was one man who was angry toward my company nearly the entire reassessment, for no apparent or rational reason. With this case, I kept my dialogue to a minimum, only asking for updates on the questions that I knew had outdated answers. When he would rant about something, I would just respond with a simple "mm" or "jeez, sorry about that, man," letting him feel heard and that I was not "corporate" so to speak. At one point, he demanded to know how much money the company received from insurance for each visit completed. I knew for a fact that no one in my office, not even the head manager, knew the answer to this. As a result, I encouraged the manager to send him to a billing specialist or someone in accounting, even just to make him feel more important and valued.

At the next job, I worked as a clinician for an Employee Assistance Program, or EAP, that provided services to some 90 companies across the county. As such, it was essential for us to have a strong provider network, and to do so honestly, making sure all of the required paperwork and documentation for each individual provider was current and organized. The main reason I was onboarded was to update credentialing for all of our employers, and to develop a system along the way that would ensure an efficient and simple way to keep everyone up to date.

If you are familiar with Microsoft Office applications, you would have probably guessed or even assumed that I utilized Excel for this undertaking. As there was no one before me who even made an attempt to gather all of the names and information for each provider in one place, I had no choice but to start from scratch. Although I am not an absolute know-it-all with Excel, or even Office in general, I know enough to help someone out that is less familiar with it. Since my department only included two other people at the time, my coworker and my boss, I became the go-to guy when it came to anything computer-related, even despite not being much of an expert on tech. Whenever my boss would encounter an issue with PowerPoint, as she presented to external clients all the time, she would either call for my help from her office or lament over having to do something frustrating.

One such time involved when an external group requested that they receive the PowerPoint slide deck after a much-appreciated presentation she put on. Immediately at this request, she stated that she was not comfortable with doing so, as each collection of slides were uniquely created for each topic, and she did not want them to go out so easily. Plus, what she did not tell them was that the department received income for each presentation that she put on, so this would potentially result in lost money. Much to her chagrin, she reluctantly agreed to provide them with the presentation's skeletal notes. Following doing so, she expressed her frustration over this to me and my coworker, as she would have to take all afternoon to manually develop the outline of this extensive presentation. It occurred to me that I had seen a way to extract an outline from a slide deck, so I told my boss to hold off and work on something else for a few minutes while I researched "something." She was confused, but went along with it. Meanwhile, I went on Google and searched for how to extract an outline from a PowerPoint presentation. Sure enough, it could be done in a few clicks of the mouse with no effort whatsoever. It didn't take but 30 seconds to walk her through the instructions and get her what she needed. I wish I could put into words the sheer joy that she expressed over this.

I can say with certain confidence how grateful I am for the lesson that the collegiate job had taught me of being willing to say, "I don't know." It is such a valuable lesson, even when you know some of what is being asked of you. I could have pretended to be the expert on PowerPoint and wasted her time hovering over her desk and walking her through misleads out of nothing but pride. Sure, this still would have saved her hours' worth of work, but probably would have resulted in more frustration for her and would have made me look like a dope. Instead, I am glad that I asked her to give me a few minutes so that I could search for the answer first.

Pride is a dangerous thing, and we all have it. If you want to be successful in college and in your respective professional field/s, do not let pride and confidence get intertwined. Always be willing to learn, accept when you have made mistakes, and do not waste the time of others in the process.

Part IV:
Author's Notes on Graduate School

As mentioned several times throughout this book, I am a mental health provider. I had the privilege of going through my undergraduate and obtaining my bachelor's degree in psychology with a minor in marketing, continuing straight through to also earn my master's degree in social work. My parents always said that it is best to continue straight through and not to wait to attend graduate school, as you get caught up in whatever job you are able to obtain with your bachelor's and life just gets ahead of you. In hindsight, they were exactly right. Returning to graduate school while working as a case manager would have been next to impossible. Having already started my master's program, I still ran into some difficult challenges to overcome. However, as hectic as that job was, I can truly not imagine how chaotic things would have been if I had to simultaneously learn how to juggle everything going on in my life.

Reflecting on what it would have been like is actually not too difficult, as my sister and my father both returned to graduate school in different ways. My sister went back about three years after she obtained her bachelor's degree. By then, she had already established herself as very reputable in a strong health care organization, and had done everything she could to climb up, even despite her young age. When given the opportunity to pursue her master's, she ran into many mountainous challenges, especially since she started graduate school during the COVID-19 pandemic. Recall that she works in health care, so you can only imagine how hectic things were as she was running vaccination clinics and overseeing several employees in the process.

My father also has a career in health care, having worked for the same organization for over 30 years. He returned to school to obtain his master's degree, as he had entered the field at a time when having a master's was less essential than it is now. This, I felt, speaks to his work ethic, as he did not necessarily need to obtain this in order to continue advancing. Nevertheless, he felt it important to do so. After 14- to 18-hour workdays, he found himself staying at his office to complete readings and homework assignments, even doing so ahead of the due date. In spite of all the pressure he was under, he still managed to pull a 4.0 GPA by the time of graduation.

The beauty of graduate school, should you decide to continue your education, is that teachers are generally more flexible and understanding that you are (likely) working full time, and are generally more willing to work with due dates. Obviously, this statement does not apply to every professor at every graduate school, though most people that I have spoken with who attended agree that this was the case for them as well. Naturally, there are exceptions to this rule. Even within my own graduate program, I had one teacher who was so tough that she was completely unwavering on anything. She turned out to be the only teacher in my entire three-year program who had an in-person test, which was not even the final exam. Before this test, she insisted that bags were left in the corner of the room, and that all pockets be emptied before sitting down. Additionally, she spaced every student apart with assigned seating to ensure that we were not in close proximity to our usual classmates.

Even with all of these tough restrictions and her tough outward appearance and demeanor, she was still a very nice person and was not difficult to work alongside. During a group project where I felt as if my team had not held up their responsibilities to the fullest extent, she was still quite happy with the final result of the class presentation and passed us with 100%. Despite the subject matter being quite difficult, and despite her being the undisputed most difficult teacher in my master's program, she was still a lot easier to work with than many of the average professors from my undergraduate experience.

This is not meant to scare you. Rather, I hope that this encourages you to consider enrolling. The workload was so much lighter, and I got the sense that the curriculum was far more focused with less filler. Personally, I enjoyed my interactions with teachers and the nature of the work overall so much more than undergraduate. This may be because I am more of a writer and less of a test-taker, and my undergraduate psychology program involved a lot of test-taking. Again, every school is different, but the nature of graduate vs. undergraduate schoolwork is consistent with whomever I speak with about their experiences.

One very big piece of advice that I want to emphasize in regard to graduate school is the importance of exploring all of your options when deciding which school to attend. There may be a knee-jerk instinct to simply enroll at your own school, thus bypassing the trouble of looking for another school. I completely understand this, as you are busy enough with everything that comes with finishing your last year of college. Plus, if you have had a positive experience at your school, it seems appealing to just continue on. There is nothing wrong with deciding to do this if you feel like your school has the best program for you. Nevertheless, if you do not explore everything that is at your disposal, you are truly missing out on trying to make this the best possible experience for yourself.

Just as different colleges and universities offer satellite campuses, online programs, part-time schedules, etc., the same goes for graduate school. Think of it like having the option to either have a pre-sewn suit or a tailor-made one. If given the same price, would you not choose the tailor-made one? Finding the program that fits the best for you is almost always an option that is not going to cost you any more. Additionally, consider any programs that would allow for reduced expenses. Some people choose to move back in with family while attending graduate school in order to not have to pay for boarding and food, saving potentially tens of thousands each year. Most graduate programs are less expensive than undergrad, so saving that much more is an excellent way to reduce your student loans, or your overall expenses if you are paying out of pocket.

If you do opt to live on campus, take the time to explore the campus and take a tour of your desired department. If you end up touring a school and you are not crazy about some of the amenities, or even just the mood overall, take your feelings into full consideration. Do not discount any concerns as petty or exaggerative. You are preparing to spend a lot of time and a lot of money on continuing your education. Do not be mistaken: searching for the right graduate school is equally as important as the process of finding an undergraduate program. Just as you did with your undergraduate program, take absolutely everything into account. Leave no stone unturned.

Similar to undergraduate school, you will join a group of other students who joined the school and/or program at the same time you did. Within graduate school, you will have enrolled and been accepted at the same time as your fellow classmates. Additionally, graduate school is a set curriculum of classes and does not include electives. In fact, you are given a strict schedule of classes based on a full-time or part-time schedule. As such, the task of meeting with an advisor or looking at your degree audit to find classes to take is a thing of the past. Rather, you are programmed into the classes you take already. This results in you being a part of what is commonly referred to as a "cohort." The basic idea of a cohort is a group of students who go through all of the classes simultaneously throughout most, if not all, of the classes in graduate school.

Earlier in the book, I mentioned the importance of connecting with like-minded classmates in your program in order to be able to collaborate with them and work on projects together. This is especially important in graduate school. The nice thing about graduate school is that everyone in your cohort is already studying within the same field as you, so you will not have to go far to find someone or some people with similar career goals as your own. Furthermore, this is actually a really great networking opportunity. By meeting everyone in your cohort and getting to know them, as well as establishing yourself as a hard and competent worker amongst them, you are developing a network of peers within your field.

Many graduate programs require some form of field placement, better known as an internship. Undergraduate programs require the same, though most graduate programs that involve a field placement require far more hours than any undergraduate program does. For instance, my undergraduate program required an internship that gathered somewhere between 60 and 80 registered hours at an approved placement. This pales in comparison to the 750 hours that I had to obtain in graduate school.

The nice part of a graduate field placement, however, is that you can find opportunities to incorporate your job into the internship if you work within a relevant field. However, between your years, you may need to take on a different role at your job, as field placements often require that students go through a new experience for each new school year. As such, it is wise to search for jobs within your field that would be willing to provide an opportunity to gain field hours and label it as an internship.

Within the field of social work, there was a recent change to the national policy for graduate internships. Gaining hours at one's current job is no longer as simple as just labeling your current work as your internship. Rather, from year to year, you have to prove that whatever your responsibilities at work involve could be labeled as a "new experience" for you that you have not already done prior to the field placement. This is one of the reasons that I was trained in so many different areas at my case management job. Doing this proved to be an excellent way to complete my field placement. Not only was I paid while gaining hours, but I was able to build extra experience and training in a way that was not allotted to my coworkers. Additionally, I did not have to commute to another destination and work additional hours (unpaid hours as well) after a long day at a very intense job. On top of all of these benefits, I am able to list all of these different experiences on my resume as if they were separate jobs, as people were hired in the company to complete one of the several areas that I was trained in. As such, I had enough experience to represent the equivalent of four to five workers.

This need for a good internship situation goes back to the need to make sure that your graduate school situation is working for you, particularly geographically. My graduate school was located a good distance from my hometown and, subsequently, my work as well. As a result, most of the suggested field placement opportunities recommended by my advisor and department overall were located at least 45 minutes from me, some even two hours. When I had initially requested that my job at the time could take the place of signing on to an external field placement, I was immediately turned down for the very reason described above: that it was not a "new experience" and that I had already been trained in my current work. Despite the job still being new for me, I had already gone through the three-month training and shadowing required to work independently, so it was an immediate "no" from the department. Since I drove all day for work, I was not prepared to drive an extra hour each way to commute to another position, especially since most field placements are not paid.

It was due to all of these factors and more that I pushed to be able to use my job as a field placement. Thankfully, my advisor was the head of the department at the time, and she was kind enough to visit my work in person to discuss this with my manager and the on-site clinician. The four of us sat down and determined that it would actually be possible to utilize my work with adults as my internship, as I worked with both children and adults at the time, and they were classified as two completely different departments within the company that required two separate training methods. We broke down the basic components of the adult program, every single bit of detail and responsibility that was involved, and were able to create a proper foundation. The clinician gladly and generously volunteered to be my field supervisor, and from there we were good to go. The following year, my organization offered to train me to complete intakes and reassessments for the child and adolescent program, which provided me with another "new experience" to gain plenty of hours. As you can probably imagine, since both of these experiences were my full-time job, gaining hours was extremely easy to do, and I never found myself having to scramble to do so. The contracts developed for my work were very straight-forward, and even warranted me working overtime on many days. I was very blessed and fortunate to be able to do this, but it would not have worked out had I not pushed and advocated for myself. Keep in mind that you are your own biggest advocate, whether in college, graduate school, or in the post-graduate life. Stand up for yourself and your rights, and make your desired outcomes happen.

Joining graduate school was somewhat unnerving for me in the beginning of it all. As mentioned, I already worked full-time at a very intense job, and I had returned to my hometown and moved back in with my parents to save on expenses. As such, I did not reside on a campus, which was a big change and transition for me. Additionally, I had opted to

143

enroll in a satellite campus about 35 minutes away from our home, so I had to commute after work to classes in the evening. The satellite campus was hardly a campus at all, more just a building in a small downtown area with a courtyard next to a public parking garage. At first, not having a beautiful campus was somewhat depressing, but the building was very nice and more modern than anything at my undergraduate school, so it did not take long to get used to this.

My cohort was rather small, only having about eight to twelve people in it at a time. You would think that all of us became pretty close. Just the opposite was true. Even within that small group, we were still quite reserved, resorting to our own new cliques. All of us got along for the most part and interacted well, but there was not much collaboration outside of the three or four clusters of students. Only in the last semester or two did most of the cohort start to collaborate, though there was naturally some power struggle as to who ought to lead.

The frustrating part of our program was that many classes were shared with undergraduate social work students, so there was often a lot of immaturity within the classes. The school offered a streamlined undergraduate program to allow students in pursuit of their bachelor's to reduce the volume of classes needed for both their bachelor's and their master's degrees. The best class environments were always the smaller ones reserved for the graduate programs, and had I known this while exploring school programs, it may very well have changed my decision. However, this was my only major complaint, and I enjoyed my program very much. This only goes to show the importance of looking at every single detail.

Go ahead and annoy the recruiter that you are in contact with. Test the limits of their knowledge. Schedule meetings with the head of your chosen department. Just when you think you have learned everything there is to know going in, you may get a curveball thrown your way. Do your best to be ready to catch it when it flies your way.

Finally, as you consider your career path for your undergraduate degree, keep in mind that the market is competitive for competent and reliable workers, but well-educated ones as well. When considering whether or not you wish to continue after obtaining your bachelor's degree, keep the competitive nature of the work world in mind as you make your decision. Yes, it is more money; and yes, it is more time. Yes, you will have to find an internship/field placement, and yes, it will take an extra year to realize your full potential within your desired field. However, it is a guaranteed way to find better work options quicker, and an incredible way to accompany your excellent work ethic in doing your best to make a desirable living for yourself.

Conclusion

Wow, it is hard to believe that the end has been reached. Just as the four main years of college fly by with all of the different, crazy things that happen, so has the journey that we have gone on together as reader and writer. Whether you skimmed this book for key points or read it cover to cover, it is my hope that you got the most out of what it has to say and offer you.

The target group that this book has in mind is that of soon-to-be college freshman; whether that means someone graduating high school or even the 8th grade. However, the subjects discussed in here have tremendous potential for someone who is already in college and needs to hit the reset button on their habits and methods. Everything was done to write in such a way that could speak to anyone, not leaving anybody out. After all, not every college student falls under the stereotypical age range of 18-21 years old.

In review, it is worth reiterating the point that has been regurgitated so many times along the way. The information and suggestions in this book are not one size fits all. Rather, everything should be taken with a grain of salt. Take what you read and see how it applies in your own life, see what components of it you find true, and what is not so much the case for you. I have done what I can to provide some examples from my college experiences, my work experiences, and my social life. All three are some of the most important facets of the typical collegiate career and, as was stated in one of the Author's Experiences, there is almost always more to learn from one's mistakes than one's successes. If this book proves to be helpful in saving trouble for at least one person out there, then it will have all been worth it.

Another hopeful key takeaway is that good habits need to be established early on in college to ensure success in both the classes that will test the limit of your sanity, as well as the work world that is not as far away as it may seem right now. Old habits die hard, and changing your ways is not some sort of a light switch that can be flipped on. It takes time, patience, development, and even failure. Taking the time that has been given to you in college to figure things out and find both enjoyment and efficiency is essential.

So much of college is about meeting new people. You have no choice but to develop socially as you encounter new professors, advisors, friends, miscellaneous school administration, classmates, group project members, etc. This really does not slow down throughout the four years, and only continues if you decide to go on to graduate school. I have done my best in discussing how to do so and manage yourself while doing so. However, I would not be doing my job if I did not also encourage you to get to know yourself. In all honesty, while development in high school is a big part of growing up, the time and personalities experienced at this point in your life are not as consistent with who we grow up to be as college is. College introduces a new level of independence, both recreational and academic—even professional. Let's be honest, I look back on the things that I enjoyed in high school and cannot help but cringe. With the new level of independence in college comes a natural shift in tastes, preferences, and hopefully a new appreciation of life in general. On top of that, you are expected to take advantage of this new independence and freedom, needing to step up to the wheel and throw your own twist into the path that you take. No one has the ability to choose your destiny except for you, so take full rein of everything at your disposal.

Finally, in writing on the subject of college, it is worth noting that you are very fortunate to have the option of pursing an education! Many people around the world, even many in this country, would give anything to be able to be in your position. Take full advantage of everything that your school has to offer, as most schools have a number of free resources, activities, events, recreational outlets, groups, and other things that are offered at no additional expense. However, never take your education for granted. Some people even decide to study abroad for a year in a country and/or culture that has always fascinated them. If this option is allotted to you, do not pass it up. I had several friends in college that chose to either study abroad for a full year or took advantage of an overseas tour over the summer. Two of my closest friends went on a European tour, visiting the majority of Europe's countries and seeing so many sights within each one. This is something that they talk about to this day, and consider to be one of the most exciting times of their lives.

Best wishes to you. Now that our journey together is through, go out and find yourself on your own journey!

Made in the USA
Middletown, DE
29 May 2021

40687200R00086